Performance, Challenges and Prospects of AKSHAYA PATRA SCHEME (PROGRAMME) IN GUJARAT

Performance, Challenges and Prospects of AKSHAYA PATRA SCHEME (PROGRAMME) IN GUJARAT

Dr. Sangeeta Ghate

ABD PUBLISHERS
Jaipur ■ New Delhi

ABD PUBLISHERS

Regd. Off. "Bony Residency", Gate No. 2
Opp. Tilak Public School, Vishweswariya Nagar,
Gopalpura Road, Jaipur - 302018, India
Ph: 0141 - 2761280, Telefax: 2761381
Email: abdpublishersjpr@gmail.com

Delhi Office: 102, 1st Floor, Satyam House,
4327/3, Ansari Road, Darya Ganj,
New Delhi - 110002, India
Ph: 011-45652440

visit us: www.oxfordbookcompany.com

Distributed By
KEYA INTERNATIONAL PRESS LLP
E-mail: keyainternationalpressllp@gmail.com

Published in India, 2025

Price: ₹ 1595/-

ISBN: 9788183766838

Typeset by Shivangi Computer, Jaipur

Printed and bound in India by Thomson Press Ltd.,
New Delhi

CONTENTS

PREFACE

We as a country are playing an increasingly prominent role in world economics and our industrial sector, particularly the services industry such as financial services and software industry, is noteworthy. Popularly called as knowledge based industry, these sectors are major contributors to our economy and help us earn recognition globally. In backdrop of this, the need for good quality education and thereby bringing up our vast work-force up-to-date with the demands and requirements of these sectors can hardly be disputed.

However, even before joining the main-stream economy, the workforce has to be properly educated. Making primary education accessible to all thus becomes the starting point to fulfilling this need and this has been one of the goals of our governments over past few years. However, often, and especially in families belonging to the lower economic strata, an additional member in family is primarily considered useful as being a helping hand for earning for the family and thus education takes a back seat – considered not a priority area. If children attended schools up to a tender age, many would drop out of studies sooner or later and join their families' bread earners.

The above notwithstanding, access to food, and especially, nutritious and good quality food, itself remained a challenge. As a result, mid-day meals to students in schools were introduced with the idea of serving dual purpose – providing good quality, nutritious meals to children thereby ensuring good health, and, by way of incentive, attract more and more students towards schools. The findings of studies and surveys carried out during the course of gathering information for this book corroborates this interesting fact.

Apart from helping achieve Universal Elementary Education, mid-day meals have the potential of achieving other Millennium Development Goals such as help bridge gender inequality gap and reduce the proportion of those who suffer from hunger.

Providing mid-day meals began with providing raw material, grains etc. to schools and cooking in the backyards of schools and classrooms. This, however, was full of many pitfalls and challenges and thus services of external agencies were roped in which helped ensure good quality, consistency, maintaining hygiene along with monitor-ability of the entire process.

Akshaya Patra Foundation is one such key participant and stake-holder of the Mid-Day Meals Scheme. Through surveys and analysis of data so gathered, the book attempts to get an insight into the performance and success of the Mid-Day Meals Scheme itself and in particular, that of Akshaya Patra as a role model.

Bringing out a study and publishing it as a book, I found out, can be daunting, especially when coupled with academic and administrative responsibilities. Without the help of my team who helped gathering information at field level and interacting with schools and other participants of survey my work could not have begun. I would like to sincerely thank them all for their dedicated efforts.

I am also grateful and indebted towards my family for the encouragement I have received during the course of my work and am delighted to dedicate this book to them.

— **Dr. Sangeeta Ghate**

1

INTRODUCTION

The UNDP report "India and the Millennium Development Goals" dated February 2015 suggests that the country is on-track to achieve its hunger reduction targets. Accelerated economic progress in recent years has put us on-track to achieve halving hunger target just after the 2015 deadline. Nevertheless, India continues to remain home to one quarter of the world's undernourished population, over a third of the world's underweight children. Hunger leads to sluggish growth and requires complementary interventions in several other areas. India State Hunger Index (ISHI) reported that, "India is home to the world's largest food insecure population, with more than 200 million people who are hungry." Adding to this, the report urged that, the country's poor performance is driven by its high levels of child under-nutrition and poor calorie count. Poverty is a critical issue which has its adverse impact on the nutritional level of the children and their educational attainment. The socio-economic factors present in the society lead most of the children to suffer from under nutrition, more often they drop out from schools at an early age which directly affects the progress of the nation. School feeding programme is a direct approach to improve the nutritional status of children as well as for rapidly and effectively increasing students' attendance in schools.

Immediate action to ensure that India accelerates its progress on curbing hunger is to step up and incorporate improvements into the targeted child nutrition programmes such as the Integrated Child Development Services (ICDS) scheme, and other programmes relevant to children, such as the National Rural Health Mission (NRHM, now known as the NHM), the Scheme for Empowerment of Adolescent Girls-SABLA, the Public Distribution System (PDS) and sanitation programmes. The implementation of National Food Security Act should also be expedited by completing targeting and identification of intended beneficiaries to ensure that poor people get affordable access to healthy and nutritious food.

Education and child health are important tools of poverty reduction and economic development. With the recent focus on Universal Elementary Education as a Millennium Development Goal, many developing countries have made dramatic improvements in school enrolment and attendance rate. School feeding programmes have, in theory, the potential to contribute to at least three Millennium Development Goals: to reduce the proportion who suffer from hunger (Goal 1) and are underweight; to help achieve universal primary education (Goal 2); and to promote gender equality (Goal 3) through effects on school enrolment, attendance and retention.

The National Programme of Nutritional Support, popularly known as Mid-Day Meal Scheme is the largest social welfare programme in India. It involves provision of lunch, free of cost to school-going children on all working days. Presently in India, 12Crore students of 12 Lakh schools are getting benefit under this programme.

OBJECTIVES OF MID-DAY MEAL SCHEME

The National Programme of Nutritional Support to Primary Education, popularly known as Mid-Day Meal Scheme was launched in India on 15th August 1995, with the main objectives of –

- Boosting Universalization of Primary Education by increasing enrolment, retention and attendance.

- Improving the Nutritional Status of children studying in class I-V and class VI-VIII.
- Accelerating the process of socialization.
- Encouraging poor children, belonging to disadvantaged sections, to attend schools regularly and help them concentrate on classroom activities.
- Providing nutritional support to children of primary stage in drought-affected areas during summer vacation.

Mid-Day MealPrograms (school lunch) emerged to address the multiple challenges of poverty, hunger, and access to education. Prior to receiving mid-day meals, many impoverished children performed poorly in school due to short attention spans associated with extreme hunger. Other children either did not enroll in school, or dropped out at a young age choosing to seek work during the school day to earn money to feed themselves and their families.

Although 50 percent of India's children were malnourished, the provision of mid-day meals was sporadic and in many places non-existent. Responding to pressure from the Indian people, theSupreme Court of India passed an order on November 28, 2001, which mandated: "Cooked mid-day meal is to be provided in all the government and government-aided primary schools in all the states."

Inconsistent food quality, occasional food poisoning, poor hygiene, and operational concerns were among the complications to the provision of government-sponsored mid-day meals. The meals were prepared by teachers, who cooked the same meal every day: *ghoogri,* gruel made of boiled wheat. Children reported that they grew tired of eating the same food daily, they did not like the taste, and it often made them feel sick. In 2004, a fire accidentally started by a teacher cooking the mid-day meal killed 90 children in Tamil Nadu, an event which underscored the safety issues inherent in meals prepared in makeshift kitchens based on school sites.

As a budgetary allocation, India remains a country with limited spending on health (India's public health expenditure as a percentage of GDP is only 4%, when compared to the highly developed nations which spend nearly 9-10% of their GDP on health), as per figures released by World Bank in the Human Development Report for 2015. The Indian data on states (though a bit dated) cites Gujarat as spending 0.57% of its GDP on health as per the Indian Human Development report (2011), with public expenditure contributing towards 20.8% of the total health expenditure (while the national average is much higher at 28%). In such budgetary constraints, the impact that funds leveraged through CSR and role of NGOs can create has a huge need.

AKSHAYA PATRA

In 2000, The Akshaya Patra Foundation (TAPF) was founded to address the dual challenges of hunger and education in India. The organization provided nutrition-rich mid-day meals to extremely underprivileged children in India with the aim of increasing school enrolment, reducing drop-out rates, and improving academic performance. The AkshayaPatraprogram had a simple vision: "No child in India should be deprived of education because of hunger." Because of India's enormous population, this vision was difficult to realize.

Akshaya Patra began feeding 1,500 students in five schools in Bangalore. It was one of the first organizations in the region to provide freshly cooked, hot and nutritious, balanced meals, and within six months of starting the program, it had requests from 3,000 schools. Akshaya Patra soon scaled up services to feed 30,000 children. When the Foundation's growth caught the attention of local government officials, the organization began receiving government financial support. By April 2003, it was feeding 43,000 children in Bangalore daily.

In 2001, a cooked mid-day meal became a right for children studying in schools run or aided by the Government when the Supreme Court of India passed an interim order on the Mid-Day Meal Scheme (MDMS), and directed the Governments of all States and Union Territories to implement it. The Akshaya Patra Foundation, in 2003, became the first organization to forge a

Public – Private Partnership with the Government to implement the Mid-Day Meal Scheme after it signed anMoU with the Government of Karnataka for AksharaDasoha.

To fulfill the dream, committed and like-minded individuals embarked on this journey under the leadership of MadhuPanditDasa. The first delivery vehicle was donated by Mohandas Pai while Abhay Jain promised to bring in more donors. Soon, they realized that the initiative had a two-fold success – it served as an incentive for children to come to school, and also helped them concentrate on their studies. Becoming a beacon of change in the society, the Foundation set forth its operations, and has been an example of good governance, prudent financial reporting and an admirable Public - Private Partnership, in turn, contributing to nation building. Everyone involved with the cause has always been conscious of the huge responsibility that lay with every step taken. Akshaya Patra has always pursued financial transparency in the sector. In 2008, the Foundation became the first NGO to adhere to the International Financial Reporting Standards.

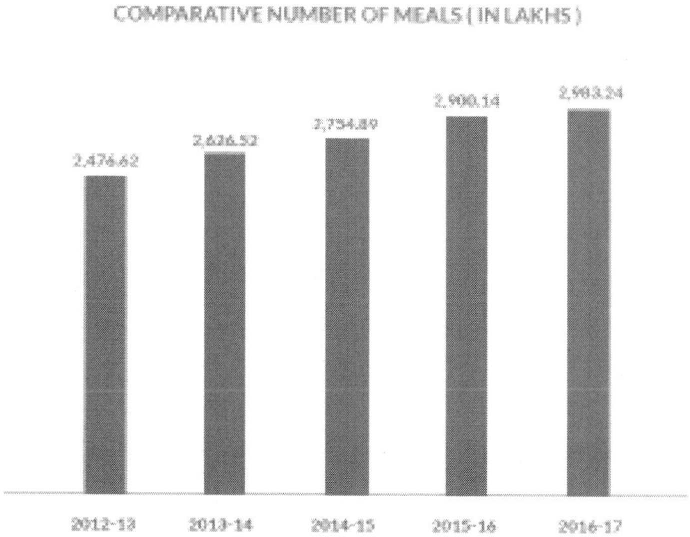

Figure 1: Comparative - No. of Meals

In 2013, the organization entered the Institute of Chartered Accountants of India's (ICAI) Hall of Fame after receiving the Institute's Gold Shield Award for Excellence in Financial Reporting for the fifth consecutive year. As a responsive organization, by means of feeding millions of children, Akshaya Patra aims to contribute in nation building and also to achieve the two most critical UN Sustainable Development Goals: Zero Hunger and Quality Education.

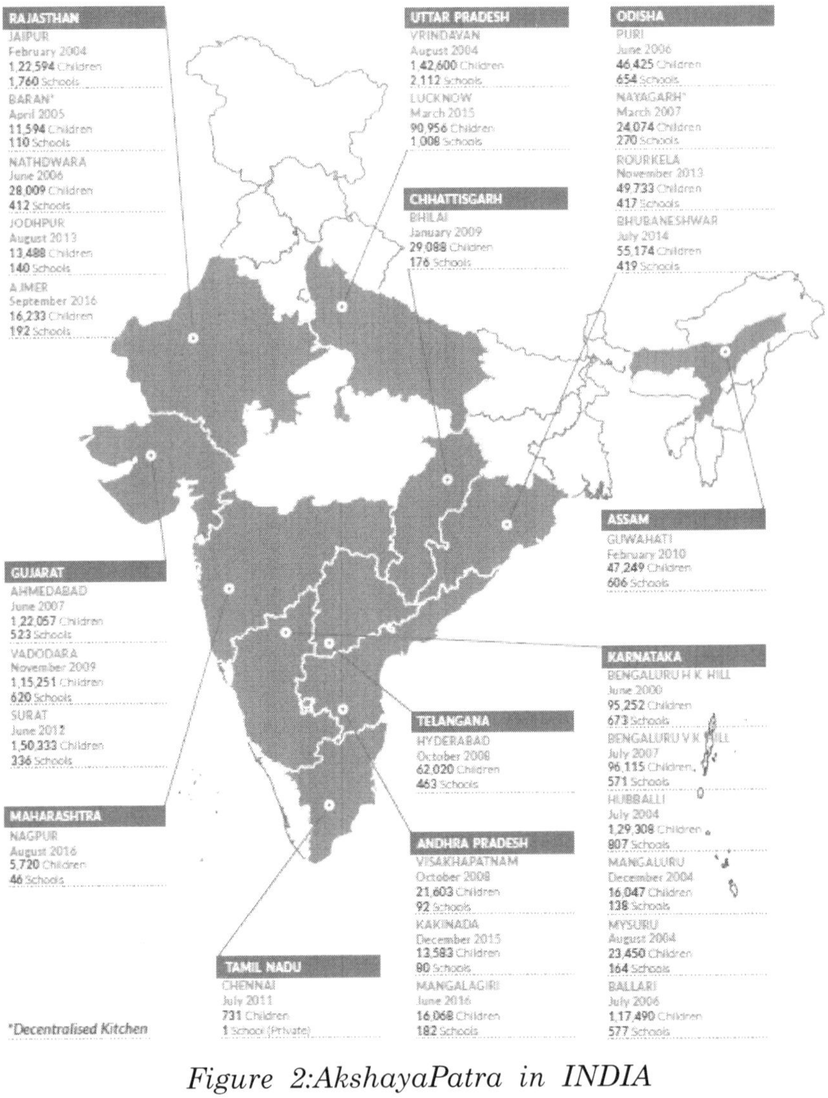

Figure 2:AkshayaPatra in INDIA

The Foundation serves mid-daymeal to 1.66 million children in 13,549 schools across 11 states. In order to feed millions of children, Akshaya Patra depends on its centralized and decentralized kitchen units; centralized kitchens — courtesy the latest technology — can prepare up to 100,000 meals in few hours. Akshaya Patra opened three new kitchens at Nagpur, Maharashtra; at Mangalagiri, Andhra Pradesh and at Ajmer, Rajasthan. The Foundation now caters to 27 locations with 26 centralized and 2 decentralized kitchens. AkshayaPatra's first decentralized kitchen was started in April 2005 in Baran, Rajasthan when it was realized that the terrain made it difficult for a centralized kitchen to operate efficiently. Women's self-help groups were appointed to run small kitchens thus promoting women empowerment and gender parity.

Each of these kitchens served one or two schools and was monitored by the organization. The same system was introduced in Nayagarh, Odisha, in March 2007. Akshaya Patra commemorated the serving of 2 billion cumulative meals in the august presence of the President of India, ShreePranab Mukherjee. A precursor to the mission to reach five million children by 2020, the Foundation adheres to the belief of continuous improvement and going that extra mile to bring smiles on children's faces.

CENTRALIZED KITCHENS

A centralized kitchen helps to manage operations from a single point of control; this includes receiving, storage, preparation, delivery and maintenance, among other processes that form the cycle of mid-daymeal operations. Currently, 31 centralized kitchens operate in 12 states of India and these kitchens prepare mid-day meals for 16,40,012 school children.

Figure 3: CentralizedKitchen at Akshaya Patra

The Akshaya Patra centralized kitchens are equipped with cauldrons, trolleys, rice chutes, *dal/sambar* tanks, cutting boards, knives and other similar equipment that are sanitized before usage. The semi-automated kitchens have the capacity to undertake large scale feeding, typically up to 100,000 mid-day meals a day and they also adhere to Food Safety Management Systems (FSMS) to ensure safe handling, preparation and delivery of the food.

Using these highly mechanized units, Akshaya Patra is able to achieve the highest levels of hygiene by reducing human contact with the food. After cooking, the food is packed into stainless steel containers and transported via conveyor belts to be loaded into custom made food distribution vehicles, to be taken to the beneficiary schools.

DECENTRALIZED KITCHENS

Decentralized kitchens are set up in locations where geographical terrain and bad road connectivity make it difficult to set up a large infrastructure. These kitchens are run by women

Self-Help Groups (SHGs) who undertake the cooking process under the guidance of Akshaya Patra. The members of these groups are trained in AkshayaPatra's kitchen processes and operations module and are monitored by Akshaya Patra representatives to ensure that safe, nutritious food is being provided to children in their mid-day meal.

Figure 4: Women Self-Help Groups (SHGs)

Akshaya Patra has decentralized kitchens in Baran, Rajasthan reaching out to 155 schools and in Nayagarh, Odisha reaching out to 342 schools. Akshaya Patra set up our first decentralized kitchen in Baran, Rajasthan and with support from the local Sarpanch (head of the village) of the area, Akshaya Patra hired and trained women from Self-Help Groups to cook the nutritious food in kitchens across the district, and feed the children.

While the decentralized kitchens prepare mid-day meals for school children, they also help in building Self-Help Groups with sustainable income and social standing.

2

LITERATURE REVIEW

INDIA AND MALNUTRITION

Malnutrition refers to the situation where there is an unbalanced diet in which some nutrients are in excess, lacking or wrong proportion. Simply put, we can categorize it to be under-nutrition and over-nutrition. Despite India's 50% increase in GDP since 1991, more than one third of the world's malnourished children live in India. Among these, half of them under 3 are underweight and a third of wealthiest children are over-nutrient.

The World Bank estimates that India is one of the highest ranking countries in the world for the number of children suffering from malnutrition. The prevalence of underweight children in India is among the highest in the world, and is nearly double that of Sub Saharan Africa with dire consequences for mobility, mortality, productivity and economic growth.

The 2017 Global Hunger Index (GHI) Report ranked India 97th out of 118 countries with a serious hunger situation. Amongst South Asian nations, it ranks third behind only Afghanistan and Pakistan with a GHI score of 29.0.

India is one of the fastest growing countries in terms of population and economics, sitting at a population of 1.342 billion and growing at 1.5%–1.7% annually (from 2001–2007).India's Gross Domestic Product growth was 9.0% from 2007 to 2008; since Independence in 1947, its economic status has been classified as a low-income country with majority of the population at or below the poverty line.

Though most of the population is still living below the National Poverty Line, its economic growth indicates new opportunities and a movement towards increase in the prevalence of chronic diseases which is observed in at high rates in developed countries such as United States, Canada and Australia. The combination of people living in poverty and the recent economic growth of India has led to the co-emergence of two types of malnutrition: under nutrition and over nutrition.

Some of the major causes for malnutrition in India are Economic inequality. Due to the low social status of some population groups, their diet often lacks in both quality and quantity. Women who suffer malnutrition are less likely to have healthy babies. In India, mothers generally lack proper knowledge in feeding children. Consequently, new born infants are unable to get adequate amount of nutrition from their mothers. Deficiencies in nutrition inflict long-term damage to both individuals and society.

Gujarat

Gujarat is situated on the west coast of India. It is bounded in the west by the Arabian Sea, in the north-west by Pakistan, in the north by Rajasthan, in the east by Madhya Pradesh and in the south and south-east by Maharashtra. The state of Gujarat occupies the northern extremity of the western sea-board of India. It has the longest coast line of 1290 kilometers.

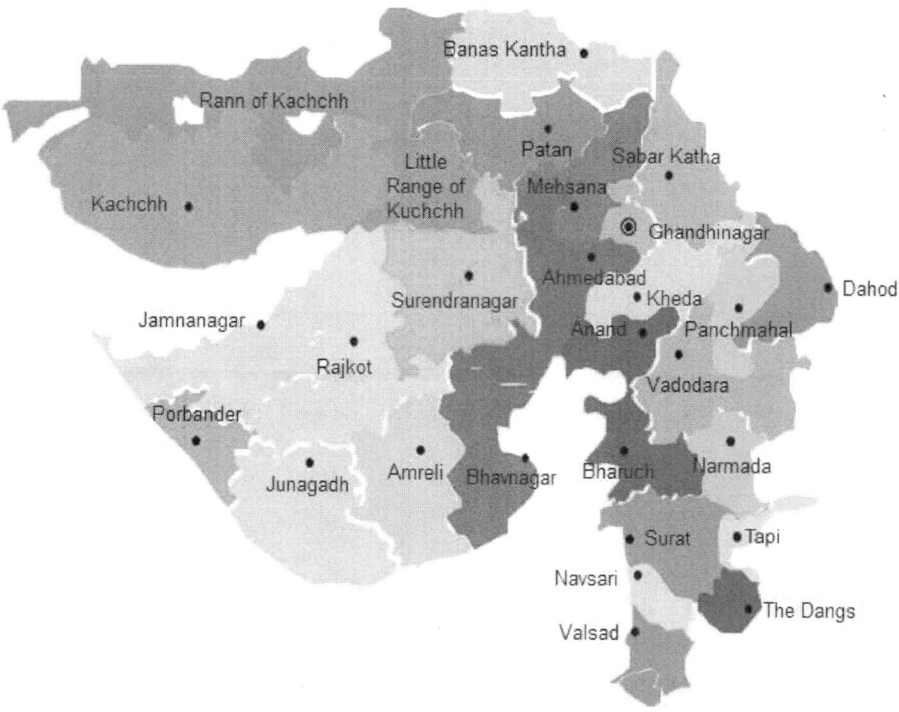

Figure 5: Map of Gujarat

The state comprises of three geographical regions. The peninsula, traditionally known as Saurashtra, is essentially a hilly tract sprinkled with low mountains. Kutch on the north-east is barren and rocky and contains the famous Rann (desert) of Kutch, the big Rann in the north and the little Rann in the east. The mainland extending from the Rann of Kutch and the Aravalli Hills to the river Damanganga is on the whole a level plain of alluvial soil.

Nutrition data generated from the fourth National Family Health Survey (NFHS-4) conducted in 2015-16 are now available for all Indian States/Union Territories. The following inferences may be drawn from the data on nutritional status presented in Table 1;the nutritional status of children under five years is critical in the States/UTs of Bihar, Jharkhand, Uttar Pradesh, and Dadra and Nagar Haveli; Kerala and Mizoram are faring better.

Table 1 Nutrition Status of Indian Population, by State/ UT, 2015-16

State / Union Territory	Children (under 5 years)			
	Stunted	Wasted	Underweight	Anemic (6-59 months)
A & N Islands-UT	23.3	18.9	21.6	49
Andhra Pradesh	31.4	17.2	31.9	58.6
Arunachal Pra.	29.4	17.3	19.5	50.7
Assam	36.4	17	29.8	35.7
Bihar	48.3	20.8	43.9	63.5
Chandigarh-UT	28.7	10.9	24.5	73.1
Chhattisgarh	37.6	23.1	37.7	41.6
Daman & Diu-UT	23.4	24.1	26.7	73.8
D & N Haveli-UT	41.7	27.6	38.9	84.6
Delhi NCT-UT	32.3	17.1	27	62.6
Goa	20.1	21.9	23.8	48.3
Gujarat	**38.5**	**26.4**	**39.3**	**62.6**
Haryana	34	21.2	29.4	71.7
Himachal Pra.	26.3	13.7	21.2	53.7
Jammu &Kashm.	27.4	12.1	16.6	43.3
Jharkhand	45.3	29	47.8	69.9
Karnataka	36.2	26.1	35.2	60.9
Kerala	19.7	15.7	16.1	35.6
Lakshadweep-UT	27	13.8	23.4	51.9
Madhya Pradesh	42	25.8	42.8	68.9
Maharashtra	34.4	25.6	36	53.8
Manipur	28.9	6.8	13.8	23.9
Meghalaya	43.8	15.3	29	48

Mizoram	28	6.1	11.9	17.7
Nagaland	28.6	11.2	16.8	21.6
Odisha	34.1	20.4	34.4	44.6
Punjab	25.7	15.6	21.6	56.6
Puducherry-UT	23.7	23.6	22	44.9
Rajasthan	39.1	23	36.7	60.3
Sikkim	29.6	14.2	14.2	55.1
Tamil Nadu	27.1	19.7	23.8	50.7
Telangana	28.1	18	28.5	60.7
Tripura	24.3	16.8	24.1	48.3
Uttarakhand	33.5	19.5	26.6	59.8
Uttar Pradesh	46.3	17.9	39.5	63.2
West Bengal	32.5	20.3	31.5	54.2
India	**38.4**	**21**	**35.7**	**58.4**

Source:*Ministry of Health and Family Welfare. NFHS-4. 2015-16. All-India and State/UT Fact Sheets. Mumbai: IIPS.*

Gujarat's performance (or more appropriately, lack of performance) is particularly striking as it is one of the wealthiest states in India in terms of state per capita GNP. As we see in the Table, Gujarat is the 8th, 3rd and 5th highest percentages in stunted, wasted and underweight children.

More than 1.45 lakh children under the age of six years in Gujarat have been identified with the worst category of malnutrition — Severe Acute Malnutrition (SAM), according to state health officials. So far, 43 lakh children, the estimated number in the age group in Gujarat, have been screened as part of a government's campaign to improve the situation. Reflecting the acute problem of malnutrition in Gujarat, the state government's own programme *KuposhanMukt Gujarat MahaAbhiyan* which was launched on May 24,2015 by Chief Minister Anandiben Patel in tribal district of Chhota Udepur — revealed the alarming number of children suffering from SAM (The Times of India, 2015).

The below graph shows the prevalence of malnutrition among children <5 years across the six administrative divisions in Gujarat, as per Comprehensive Nutrition Survey in Gujarat (CNSG), conducted under the aegis of the Women & Child Development, Govt. of Gujarat in 2014.

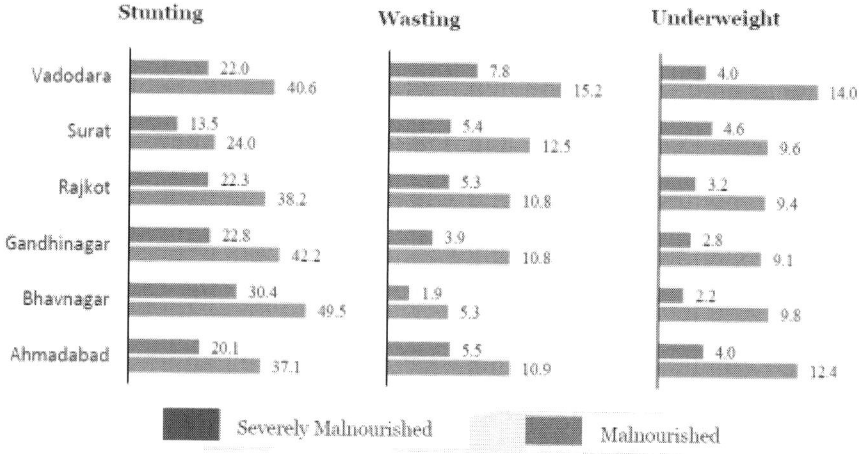

Figure 6: Malnutrition Related Data for Major Cities of Gujarat

As per the Comprehensive Nutrition Survey in Gujarat (CNSG, 2014)

- Around 12% infant and young children fed with minimum dietary diversity. Junk food and low nutritional value foods were commonly given to the children 6 to 35 months.
- 39% children were not receiving any service from ICDS and AWC. Only 40% children aged between 36-59 months were going to the AWC. 40% children aged 6-59 months were receiving take home ration.
- In 2014, prevalence of underweight (too thin for age) in Gujarat is estimated to be at 10.4% whereas wasting (too thin for height) is estimated to be at 11.4%. Stunting (too short for age) is estimated to be at 37.2%.

The district-wise data on nutrition status of children, as per as per Women and Child Development Department (MPR- March 2016), Gujarat indicate that Dang, Tapi and Surat districts have the highest proportion of severely underweight children in Gujarat.

Table 2 District-wise data on nutrition status of children

S/N	Districts	Nutrition Status (no.)				Nutrition Status (%)			
		Normal	Moderately Underweight	Severely Underweight	Total Under-weight	% of Normal	% of Mod. Under wt.	Severely Underweight	% of Total Under-weight
1	Ahmedabad	2,62,835	13,077	2,108	15,185	94.54	4.7	0.76	5.46
2	Amreli	94,326	2,729	560	3,289	96.63	2.8	0.57	3.37
3	Banaskantha	2,72,259	8,480	984	9,464	96.64	3.01	0.35	3.36
4	Vadodara	1,13,977	10.404	1,121	11,525	90.82	8.29	0.89	9.18
5	Bharuch	1,02,307	3,664	488	4,152	96.1	3.44	0.46	3.9
6	Narmada	44,806	4,978	436	5,414	89.22	9.91	0.87	10.78
7	Bhavanagar	1,46,721	11,013	1,969	12,982	91.87	6.9	1.23	8.13
8	Dang	19,940	5,199	460	5,659	77.89	20.31	1.8	22.11
9	Jamnagar	72,954	5,066	954	6,020	92.38	6.41	1.21	7.62
10	Junaghadh	92,117	2,120	446	2,566	97.29	2.24	0.47	2.71
11	Porbandar	32,405	670	199	869	97.39	2.01	0.6	2.61
12	Kachh	1,81,992	423	149	572	99.69	0.23	0.08	0.31
13	Mahesana	1,25,458	1,681	182	1,863	98.54	1.32	0.14	1.46
14	Patan	83,518	8,377	864	9,241	90.04	9.03	0.93	9.96
15	Panchamahals	1,32,321	9,910	1,369	11,279	92.15	6.9	0.95	7.85

16	Dahod	2,44,917	11,316	1,162	12,478	95.15	4.4	0.45	4.85
17	Rajkot	1,26,564	2,674	553	3,227	97.51	2.06	0.43	2.49
18	Sabarkantha	1,06,446	5,715	488	6,203	94.49	5.07	0.43	5.51
19	Surat	1,60,454	19,286	2,346	21,632	88.12	10.59	1.29	11.88
20	Surendranagar	1,04,525	6,515	1,312	7,827	93.03	5.8	1.17	6.97
21	Gandhinagar	75,826	4,767	685	5,452	93.29	5.87	0.84	6.71
22	Kheda	1,50,739	8,869	939	9,808	93.89	5.52	0.58	6.11
23	Anand	1,49,992	2,459	388	2,847	98.14	1.61	0.25	1.86
24	Valsad	1,09,124	4,844	669	5,513	93.49	4.15	0.57	4.72
25	Navsari	66,599	1,335	288	1,623	97.62	1.96	0.42	2.38
26	Tapi	44,078	4,932	799	5,731	88.49	9.9	1.6	11.51
27	Botad	52,362	762	140	902	98.31	1.43	0.26	1.69
28	Morbi	52,775	1,956	314	2,270	95.88	3.55	0.57	4.12
29	Mahisagar	86,185	5,204	497	5,701	93.8	5.66	0.54	6.2
30	Girsomanath	98,026	1,780	377	2,157	97.85	1.78	0.38	2.15

31	Devbhumi Dwarka	59,370	2,600	464	3,064	95.09	4.16	0.74	4.91
32	Chhotaudepur	78,058	9,259	842	10,101	88.54	10.5	0.96	11.46
33	Aravali	78,391	3,865	337	4,202	94.91	4.68	0.41	5.09
State Total		36,22,367	1,85,929	24,889	2,10,818	94.45	4.85	0.65	5.5

The above table also indicates that Narmada, Tapi, Surat, Chhota Udepur and Dang have the highest percentage of total numbers of underweight.

Overview of Literature

Our understanding of child malnutrition and its relationship with cognitive functioning has grown in the last few decades. Research suggests that malnutrition alone does not cause irreversible damage to the brain but is believed to result from a complex interaction between environmental deprivation and under nutrition (Grantham-McGregor, 1995). Studies indicate that adequate nutrition can help prevent some of these undesirable outcomes. However, current research does not establish a causal relationship between malnutrition and mental development that could facilitate more direct action (Behrman, 1996). Methodological problems also constrain our understanding.

Thekdi K. et al. studied nutritional assessment among government & private school children in Gujarat showed among 366 boys and 134 girls of the study population, Mean Body Mass Index (BMI) for boys and girls were 16.55 ± 2.58 and 16.75 ± 5.44 respectively. BMI was more in the private school as compared to the government school.

Babar NF et al. studied nutritional status among children from upper & lower socio-economic class which showed only 16 (19.28%) were under-nourished, and 20 (24.10%) were at risk of being over-weight, and 10 (12.5%) were obese among Upper SE class whereas in children from lower SE class, 32 (41.03%) were underweight and 2 (2.56%) were at risk of being overweight, only 3 (3.84%) were obese.

Shri Hari G. et al. reviewed 11 research literatures and reported that overweight and obesity were prevalent among 8.5-29.0% and 1.5-7.4% respectively among school children.

Pandey S. et al. conducted a cross-sectional study which shows that the prevalence of childhood and adolescent overweight and obesity amongst children from a upper-socio-economic stratum of society has remained high at 25-30% during both the periods of the school-based study.

Sail (1970) investigated that children in rural areas were physically stunned and their diets were deficient in calories, protein, vitamin A, calcium and riboflavin. A school lunch providing cereal, legume and liberal amount of leafy vegetables could correct the basic deficiencies in the diet of school children.

CARE-INDIA (1977) examined the impact of school feeding on enrolment and attendance in Karnataka and found that the mean percentage of attendance increased. Absenteeism not only decreased but the Mid-Day Meal Scheme also produced stability in attendance and increased the enrolment rate by 4%.

Yeli (1979) reported that most of the pre-primary schools in Karnataka did not have their own buildings and the situation was even more acute in the rural schools and those in hill stations. Almost all the schools did not possess playground, garden and modern amenities necessary for any pre-primary school. Many schools did not have proper facilities for indoor activities and library facility for teachers. Mid-day meals were provided for children in the schools while the provision of milk existed in the schools in hill stations and in the urban schools.

NCERT (1981-82) conducted a study on 13 States implementing CARE supported Mid-Day Meal Scheme to access the impact of Mid-DayMeal Scheme in terms of increase in school enrolment and reduction in drop-out and repetition rates of the children. The study came out with conclusions that the policy on coverage of Mid-Day Meal Scheme(MDM) varied from State to State. This variation had important bearing on the relationship between total enrolment rate/ line enrolment rate and percentage of beneficiaries. Some States had their own Mid-Day Meal Schemes, apart from CARE supported programme. There was evidence that Mid-Day Meal Scheme helped in bringing more children to schools. Retention of girls and SC/ST children at the primary stage was lower than total retention. Retention rates were more strongly related to socio-economic variables than educational variables. Impact of Mid-Day Meal Scheme on Retention Rates of SC/ST

(RRS) was not evidenced. However, RRS means in Karnataka had higher values for higher intensity of Mid-Day Meal Scheme.

Rao (1983) found overall significant improvement in attendance and deterioration in academic standards after the introduction of Mid-Day Meal Scheme.

Levinger (1994) has studied the impact of School Feeding Programmes (SFPs) on school attendance, enrolment and performance. The stud\' revealed that comparison was made between fed and non-fed schools under fifteen programmes in Columbia, Kenya and the Philippines. SFP was found to be "effective on attendance" in three programmes. In ten programmes, SFP was considered "probably effective on attendance" and in the remaining two programmes, SFP was considered "ineffective on attendance". School Feeding Programmes are more effective in stable, poorer and rural areas. Impact of any School Feeding Programme is a function of the interaction between the environment in which it operates and the features incorporated into its design. SFPs can reach their full potential for stimulating cognitive development only when they are developed as part of a broader intervention to address developmental lap or deficiencies in students. Where SFPs can be designed to have an impact on nutritional status, impact on attendance and performance will be achieved. School aged child's nutritional status exerts significant influence on his academic performance.

A study in 1994 providing extracts from evaluation of the improved Mid-Day Meal Scheme in Gujarat concluded that nearly 75% of the school goers in slums from Vadodara were affected with protozoal (E. histolytica) infections and/or helminthic (round worm) infections. The former was about 50-55% and the latter 22-55%. The findings clearly indicated that blanket de-worming is a must for these under privileged school goers whether or not the State has a Mid-Day Meal Scheme.

National Council of Educational Research and Training (2000)reported that the noon meal scheme of Tamil Nadu and supply of food grains in Uttar Pradesh, have helped to improve the enrolment and retention of girls in schools.

Upadhyay (2003) found that locating *anganwadi*in primary school was found very effective and enrolment and retention of children in primary classes got a boost with linkage between ECCE and primary education.

Misra and Behera (2004) conducted a study entitled, 'Child nutrition and primary education: a comparative study of Mid-Day Meal Scheme in Orissa and Tamil Nadu' and reported that between pre-MDM period (1989-90 to 1994-95) and post-MDM period (1995-96 to 1998-99), there was an improvement in average annual growth rate of enrolment, percentage point increase in attendance and retention rate, and percentage point decline in drop-out rate in post-MDM period in Orissa as compared to Tamil Nadu, where all the parametric functions of education were on the favourable side due to long existence of the programme (since 1956). Inspite of the educational development realized through Mid-Day Meal Scheme, several socio-cultural, administrative, managerial and financial factors affected the Scheme's effectiveness in both States. It is widely accepted that it would be unwise to scrap the national programme altogether as suggested by certain sectors. However, downsizing the programme through appropriate organizational and operational measures is being considered. There is also a strong belief that though different preschool nutritional programmes can be merged among themselves, there is very little room for merging them with Mid-Day Meal Scheme. The preschool and primary school nutritional programmes are to continue as separate programmes for the benefit of the children.

CUTS (2007) studied the implementation of Mid-Day Meal Scheme in Rajasthan and found initially, students were distributed boiled wheat supplemented with groundnut and *jaggery (gur)* under the Mid-Day Meal Scheme. More than 90% parents and students were satisfied with the Mid-Day Meal Scheme. Each school is required to send a monthly expenditure statement and vouchers to the PanchayatSamiti, which is supposed to reimburse the amount within 15 days. Only 21% of the schools received the funds every month, in time. The rest got funds in a time ranging from 2 to 6 months (12% got funds once in 6 months). 97% of the teachers reported that they received good quality food grains

Mid-Day Meal Scheme and only 23% of the schools were able to receive food grains after getting them weighed before delivery. The absence of a weighing mechanism in most schools makes it difficult to measure the quantity of food grains delivered. Most schools lack adequate cooking and storage facilities. 62% of the cooks interviewed said that the mid da\' meal was cooked in the open, which is unhygienic. Teachers are spending close to 20% of their teaching time or more on managing Mid-Day Meal Scheme instead of teaching.

Deodhar (2007) in his article 'Mid-Day Meal Scheme: Understanding Critical Issues with Reference to Ahmadabad City' pointed out that Gujarat started the Mid-Day Meal Scheme in 1984 and was the only State after Tamil Nadu to start it so early. The objective was to provide one meal a day to students studying in primary classes (I-VII). It was suggested that providing nutrition bars (or perhaps a local version like chikki) and fruits like banana could be considered as one of the menus on a couple of days. This will add variety and assured nutrition to the kids. It may seem that providing nutrition bars, especially the branded ones, may turn out to be an expensive proposition. However, if these bars are supplied in large quantities, economies of scale may reduce costs. Moreover, branded nutrition bars (say of ITC) could be provided only a couple of times a week, complemented by locally made items such as *chikki* on some other days.

Parikh and Yasmeen (2004) reported that free Mid-Day meals for school students were first introduced in a Japanese private school in the late 1800s, in Brazil in the year 1938 and in the United States in the year 1946. Seeing the experiences of countries like Brazil, the United States and Japan, the Mid-Day Meal Scheme should not be discarded by the government in India.

Afridi (2005) studied the institutional and financial organization of the Mid-Day Meal Scheme in Karnataka and Madhya Pradesh. In the context of Madhya Pradesh, the report argued that the implementation of the programme is improving, but there is a lot that needs to be done, especially regarding quality of food. The new initiative of '*SuruchiBhojan* Programme' is more attractive and nutritious as it provides higher calories in comparison to the earlier *'Daliya'* Programme. Parents are more satisfied with *'SuruchiBhojan*Programme' as compared to *'Daliya'* programme. Only 30% parents preferred distribution of dry ration to the *SuruchiBhojan* programme. Parent Teacher Associations needed to be strengthened. In the context of Karnataka, the report argued that Akshara Dasoha, the Mid-Day Meal Scheme has been more planned & better managed. Iron and folic tablets as well as de-worming tablets have been regularly provided. Good community participation and School Development 85 Managing Committees are functioning well. Meals are provided regularly and quality of meal is satisfactory.

Jain G. et al. found that the magnitude of over-weight (23.8%) and obesity (8.4%) is very high and alarming for both the sex. eating habits like junk food, chocolate, eating in front of TV etc. remarkable effect on prevalence on overweight and obesity among low to high SES group. The study also suggested that under nutrition rates remain high (10.2%) in children.

The school lunch programme is become crucial to take control on malnutrition. The school lunch programme is not a recent phenomenon. At the global level, the school lunch programme was first introduced in France in the year 1885 by Victor Hugo. Since then school lunch programme was introduced in several parts of the world viz, UK (1945), USA (1946), Switzerland (1946), Japan (1947), Australia (1950), China (1964-69),and Singapore (1975). The developing countries are not an exception to the worldwide trend towards school lunch /noon-meal-programme. The programme received due attention in countries like Indonesia (1967), Thailand (1970), Korea (1973) and Samoa (1980)

Kumar (2005)in his study, 'Effectiveness of National Programme of Nutritional Support to Primary Education (MDM Scheme) in District Hamirpur of Himachal Pradesh: An Evaluative Study', concluded that minimum enrolment of students from classes I-V was found in session 2005-2006 in these selected government primary schools relative to the previous three sessions. Neither cooked nor uncooked meal has given positive indication in this direction. There is no help received on the part of local people regarding the implementation of Mid-Day Meal Scheme.

The State sponsored menu of *Kichri*and vegetable *Pulao*combination for Mid-Day Meal Scheme was totally neglected by the teachers due to heavy wastage of the meal.

Pratichi Trust (2005) conducted a study in West Bengal and found that the Mid-Day Meal Scheme was started in some 1,100 primary schools in five districts (Murshidabad, Birbhum, Bankura, Paschimb Midnapore, and Jalpaiguri) and extended to some other districts. A total of 5,200 primary schools were covered under the programme till March 31, 2004. Only a few of the richer households, mainly of caste Hindu background, were against the continuation of the MDMScheme. There were a handful of upper caste children, who in unison with their parents' inhibition towards the meal showed their disliking towards the cooked meal. Some children highlighted the need for a change in the monotonous menu of *khichuri* (made of boiled rice, pulses, turmeric, little oil and local vegetables) ever\'day. Inadequate salaries were paid to the cooks and in most of the schools, it was reported that the conversion cost was found too inadequate to make a proper meal. The scope for involving the parents in the process of implementation of the programme was very limited.

Rana (2005) in her study 'Utilization of Resources at Primary' Stage in Himachal Pradesh' revealed that in all the sampled schools there was provision of cooked Mid-Day meals. Majority of the teachers were against the Mid-Day Meal Scheme whereas, all the students were found to be satisfied with the food provided in the schools. Majority of the teachers wanted that the mid-day meal should be provided in raw form and not in cooked form. The main reason for not being in favour of Mid-Day Meal Scheme was that it is an extra burden on the teachers. Students pay more attention towards eating rather than to studies and it is very hectic to keep daily records. The suggestions given by most of the teachers for making Mid-Day Meal Scheme more effective was that either there should be separate staff for maintaining the records or this Scheme should be handed over to some other agency.

Verma (2008) studied the problems of Mid-Day Meal Scheme in elementary schools of Shimla district of Himachal Pradesh and found that after the introduction of Mid-Day Meal Scheme at elementary level most of the problems have increased at variouslevels. There was no adequate infrastructure available in the elementary schools for preparation of mid-day meals.

ANI (2009) reported that Mid-Day Meal Scheme has been successful in Uttar Pradesh in getting the rural young boys and girls to attend schools.

Nielsen in Impact Assessment of (TAPF) Mid-Day Meal Scheme concluded that the Akshaya Patra Mid-Day Meal Scheme was initiated in Hyderabad in October 2008, prior to this,government or other NGO sponsored mid-day meal was available in almost all schools. So initial impact of the programme on school enrolment and school retention was not visible in Hyderabad, but the programme has raised the average attendance in the school and attendance rate for both boys and girls has improved in last academic year.

Teachers, students and parents felt that mid-daymeal has a positive impact on school attendance and helps to bring children from marginalized community to school every day. Performance of students depicts a positive outcome for TAPF students in comparison to Non-TAPF students which suggest better attention span of TAPF students. Overall Nutritional status of TAPF students is better in comparison to Non-TAPF students. TAPF Mid-DayMeal Scheme was able to meet the classroom hunger as most of the students reported getting stomach full of meal every day. Both teachers and parents reported that clean healthy and hygienic food has been served through TAPF Mid-Day Meal Scheme however taste of the meal was reported as a concern and students and the teachers felt the taste of food and variation in menu is not completely satisfactory. Hand washing before taking meal was practiced; however it was mostly done only with water. Availability of standard plates was found as a major concern in case of Telangana.

Studies reveal that Asian Countries like Bangladesh, Indonesia and Pakistan have further gone a step ahead in providing food support to the parents of the school going children to take care of food security of the families in the form of either distribution of good grains, oil or other such food items (Panda, 2010). While in the Latin American countries of Panama, Brazil and El – Salvador food baskets, milk and cakes are provided to the school age children belonging to the slums and the disadvantaged areas in order to improve the enrolment of the schools (Moore, 1994); whereas USA has ensured the full participation of the children from the disadvantaged groups in the school by providing food packages, thus every country has considered the importance of food in improving the enrolment in schools. The school feeding programme further received a boost in 2000, as the United Nations met in Dakar to commit itself to the eradication of hunger and the attainment of universal primary education.

The genesis of mid-day meals goes back much earlier, to 1925, when the Corporation of Madras introduced the scheme for school children. Although the scheme officially started as a centrally sponsored initiative in 1995, it was limited to providing dry rations and was not fully implemented in most states until 2002. Following a Supreme Court ruling in November 2001, all State Governments were mandated to introduce cooked school meals, and by 2003 most states had started providing school meals.

Gujarat was the second state after Tamil Nadu in the country to start the MDM Scheme. In October 1984, the scheme had covered 5083 schools in 68 *talukas* out of 225*talukas* of Gujarat and from November 1984 onwards the scheme was extended to the entire state. The aim was to feed children studying in primary classes (1 to VII), with the objective of mitigating malnutrition among the vulnerable groups.

In the year 2012-2013, a total 39,123 Primary and upper primary schools, were covered under the MDM Scheme. The achievement figures for primary and upper-primary classes were 69.37% and 64.69% on 31.12.2012.

In response to the difficulties of 'on-site feeding' a new focus on delivering an appropriately-timed (with regard to effecting improvements in learning capacity) and high quality, consistent ration; the government is developing programme models that include less costly commodities and more efficient systems for the delivery of meals to school children. Drawing on the private sector and NGOs for the school feeding programme overcomes many of the difficulties of on-site preparation of meals, and may be one of the many inexpensive ways to feed children in schools. So, now the MDM Scheme initiative has been strengthened with the interventions of Private and corporate Partnerships with the Non-Government Organization (NGO) one of it being The Akshaya Patra Foundation (TAPF). This is an example of innovation in delivery of Public services through the Private Partnerships.

In a descriptive study were 50 school teachers' from 20 primary schools of Jagadhary block of district Yamunanagar were interviewed. Only 34% of teachers responded that the government has introduced mid-day meal to save children from malnutrition, universalization of primary education and to stop wastage and stagnation as the objectives of the scheme.According to the teachers, the performance of Akshaya Patra was very good and the food provided was cooked scientifically. It was hygienic, fresh and nutritious and transported in sterilized vessels.Helpers were appointed for serving the food in the schools. Co-operation from the functionaries of Akshaya Patra was appreciated and complaints and suggestions were addressed quickly. According to the teachers (99.5%), children liked the mid-day meals provided by Akshaya Patra. *Sukhadi*(79.5%), dal (70.2%) and rice (63.8%) were the most liked items by the children. Plain Roti (12.8%) and Masala Roti (17.4%) were the least liked food items.

Similar findings were seen in a study conducted to assess the implementation of Akshara Doasha programme in Hubli. They reported that the most liked food item was rice, *sambar* provided by a non-religious organization and rice, *sambar* and curd provided by religious organization as they ranked these food items to be first (1). Similarly a study conducted in Delhi, [10] also reported that children loved dal *chawal, chhole-chawal and pooris* in comparison to other menu, supplied in the MDM Scheme.Teachers were asked about what quantity of meal should be given to the children as per the MDM Scheme. Only 16.4% could not write about the calorific norms of mid-day meals. However, 62.5% out of those teachers could mention correctly the energy requirements for children through mid-day meals (i.e. 450 Kcal for 1st to 4th standard and 700 Kcal- 5th to 7th standard). Majority of them (83.6%) did not know the correct ration. In a study conducted in Yamunanagar, 78% of teachers knew that the ration allotted is 100g per student. Predominantly teachers were satisfied with the quantity (96.4%) and quality (88.7%) of the mid-day meals provided by Akshaya Patra. All the teachers said that provision of mid-day meals cooked in the centralized kitchen of Akshaya Patra was better than cooking mid-day meals in school. The main reason stated for this was the quality of food (65.1%) and hygiene (61.0%) maintained in Akshaya Patra. Majority of the teachers were satisfied with the quality of the food (98.5%) and cleanliness of the utensils used for bringing the food (88.7%). Almost 97.9% teachers said that they had tasted the food provided.

STATEMENT OF THE PROBLEM

Akshaya Patra scheme is working urban area of the main city of the state only. In Gujarat there only three cities still covered and one just opened in Bhavnagarbut real need of this scheme is for the rural portion of country but yet not cover. In Gujarat, Dang, Tapi and Surat districts have the highest proportion of severely underweight children and Narmada, Tapi, Surat, Chhota Udepur and Dang have the highest percentage of total underweight. This project focuses on the performance of Akshaya Patra scheme, challenges and prospects of the Akshaya Patra scheme in above said needy areas of Gujarat.

3

RESEARCH METHODOLOGY

RATIONALE OF THE STUDY

Research is considered to strive to arrive at answer to intellectual and practical problems through the application of scientific methods to the knowable universe. Research is a logical and systematic search for new and useful information on a particular topic. It is an investigation of finding, solutions to scientific and social problems through objective and systematic analysis. It is a search for knowledge, that is, a discovery of hidden truths. Here knowledge means information about matters. The information might be collected from different sources like experience, human beings, books, journals, nature, etc. A research can lead to new contributions to the existing knowledge. Only through research it is possible to make progress in a field. Research is done with the help of study, experiment, observation, analysis, comparison and reasoning. Research is in fact everywhere.It is a systematic, controlled, empirical and critical investigation of hypothetical propositions about the presumed relations among natural phenomena. Research is the process of systematic and in depth study or search of any particular topic, subject or area of investigation, blackened by the collection, compilation, presentation and interpretation of relevant details or data. In short search for knowledge through objective and systematic method of finding a solution to a problem is a research.

SCOPE OF THE STUDY

The study takes into consideration perception of teachers and students towards mid-daymeal. Researcher has chosen respondents (teacher and students) from the schools where The Akshaya Patra Foundation serves and interior area of Gujarat where The Akshaya Patra Foundation serves do not serve. Scope of the study is further limited to sample of 87 valid responses of teachers and 486 valid responses of students only.

OBJECTIVE OF THE STUDY

To evaluate performance, challenges and prospects of Akshaya Patra Scheme (program) in Gujarat.

Specific objective

1. To evaluate efficiency of the Akshaya Patra Scheme in Gujarat
2. To know perception of the children regarding Akshaya Patra Scheme in Gujarat
3. To evaluate the need of the Akshaya Patra Scheme in rural areas of Gujarat
4. To find out the challenges of Akshaya Patra Scheme for expansion of functioning
5. To find out prospects of Akshaya Patra Scheme in other part of Gujarat.
6. To evaluate the performance, quality and perception of student as well as teacher regarding mid-day meal.

Research design

The present study has been considered a combination of single cross-sectional descriptive and analytical research design; descriptive in nature due to the fact that finding is with the help of literature survey;single cross-sectional due to the fact data was collected from the respondent at one time only.

The Universe

For this research, the universe of the study consists of students and teachers who are connected with the MDM Scheme all over the Gujarat

Sampling Unit

Students and teachers who are connected with MDM Scheme in Gujarat were defined as sampling unit for the purpose of the study.

Size of the Sample

Sample size for the study consists of 87 teachers and 486 students from the school where the Akshaya Patra Foundation serves as well as interior portion of Gujarat (Narmada, Tapi, Chhota Udepur and Dang) not served by the Akshaya Patra Foundation.

Sources of Data

The study draws information from two sources i.e. primary data and secondary data.

Primary Data

To collect the primary data, questionnaires were prepared.

Secondary Data

The published Magazines, Reports, Newspapers, Books, Papers, Journals, Websites; and unpublished research work on Mid-Day Meal Scheme and Akshaya Patra, are used as secondary data sources.

Instruments for Data Collection:

Two instruments are developed - one for the teachers and another for the students. Basic information regarding MDM was recorded through starting portion of questionnaires. Then perception and opinion regarding MDM measured through 16 statements which were measured on five point scale. Lastly, awareness and need of the Akshaya Patra Foundation was measured on the nominal scale.

Statistical tools used for the data analysis

Tests which are applied:

- Basic descriptive analysis (Frequency, Mean, Standard Deviation).
- Cross tabulation
- Chi-square test
- Two independent sample test

Limitations of the Study

Any generalized idea is not correct due to variations in size, goal, and region followed. The study will use small sample from many schoolsonly and thus is not representative of entire population of Gujarat. Finally the study was restricted to a particular sample size as otherwise the study scope would have been extremely wide. Further research is needed that covers diverse towns and regions across Gujarat. Limitations of field work and research procedure apply to this research as well.

4

DATA ANALYSIS AND DISCUSSION

The Mid-Day Meal (MDM) Scheme, introduced in 53 *talukas* of Gujarat in 1962, covered the age group of 6-11 years. In 1984, the Government of Gujarat (GoG) extended the programme to the entire state, covering all the students in that age group. The scheme was discontinued during 1990-1991, and replaced by the Food for Education Programme. This programme provided 10 kilograms (kg) of food grains free-of-cost every month to children with 70 per cent attendance in school. The MDM Scheme, however, was reintroduced in January 15, 1992

In 1995, the Government of India (GoI) launched the National Programme – Nutritional Support to Primary Education (NP-NSPE) scheme – where all the children of the primary schools (run by GoI/local bodies) from Standard (Std.) I to V were given 100 grams and Std. VI to VII were given 150 grams of free foodgrains (wheat/rice) on the basis of enrollment. Gujarat was one of the pioneer states to introduce the concept of providing hot cooked mid-day meals to all children from Std. I to VII of primary schools run by the State Government and Municipal Corporations. The Government of Gujarat entrusted the work of running the MDM Scheme in Ahmedabad Municipal Corporation and Gandhinagar *taluka* to the Akshaya Patra Foundation. The Vadodara Municipal Corporation and Kalol and Mansa *talukas* of Gandhinagar district were assigned to the Akshaya Patra Foundation in October 2009.

The Akshaya Patra Foundation reaches out to over 1.7 million children in 14,173 schools, across 12 states in India. The mid-day meal in Gujarat is served through centralized kitchens. The Vadodara kitchen was established first in 2009, followed by Surat in 2012, Ahmedabad in 2014, Bhavnagar in 2017 and most recently by Kalol. The five kitchens together feed 4,07,452 children in 1,621 schools every day. All kitchens are equipped with roti making machines capable of cooking up to 40,000 *rotis* (Indian flatbread) per hour! The mid-day meal menu in Gujarat includes nutritious food like *roti*, rice, *khichdi* (lentils and rice), *dal* (lentil curry) and vegetable preparations.

Table 3 Reach of the Akshaya Patra Foundation in Gujarat

Ahmedabad (ISO 22000:2005)	1,15,578	522	Centralized Kitchen
Bhavnagar	25,546	56	Centralized Kitchen
Vadodara (ISO 22000:2005)	1,07,838	616	Centralized Kitchen
Surat (ISO 22000:2005)	1,43,293	337	Centralized Kitchen
Kalol	15,197	90	Centralized Kitchen
Gujarat	**4,07,452**	**1,621**	

Source : Website of Akshaya Patra

Performance of the Akshaya Patra Foundation in Gujarat

Table 3 above provides the performance of theAkshayaPatra Foundation in Gujarat. In short span of 8 to 9 years in Gujarat, the Akshaya Patra Foundation is serving more than 4 lac meals per day in more than 1600 schools which is commendable. This research project measures the performance of the Akshaya Patra

Foundation in Gujarat through recording and comparing the responses of teachers and students regarding mid-day meals in schools served by the Akshaya Patra Foundation and those served by agencies other than the Akshaya Patra Foundation.

Response of Teachers

There are total 87 teachers surveyed in this project. Out of total, 48 teachers belong to schools where the Akshaya Patra Foundation provides the mid-daymeal and remaining 39 teachers belong to schools where mid-day meals provided by others and not the Akshaya Patra Foundation.

Figure 7 provides the informative on the involvement of the teachers in the Mid-Day Meal Scheme directly or the indirectly. Majority of the teachers, around 52%, said yes, they are involved in program whereas 25% said that they are involved only sometimes. This providesa good insight that majority of the teachers are directly or indirectly involved in Mid-Day Meal Scheme.

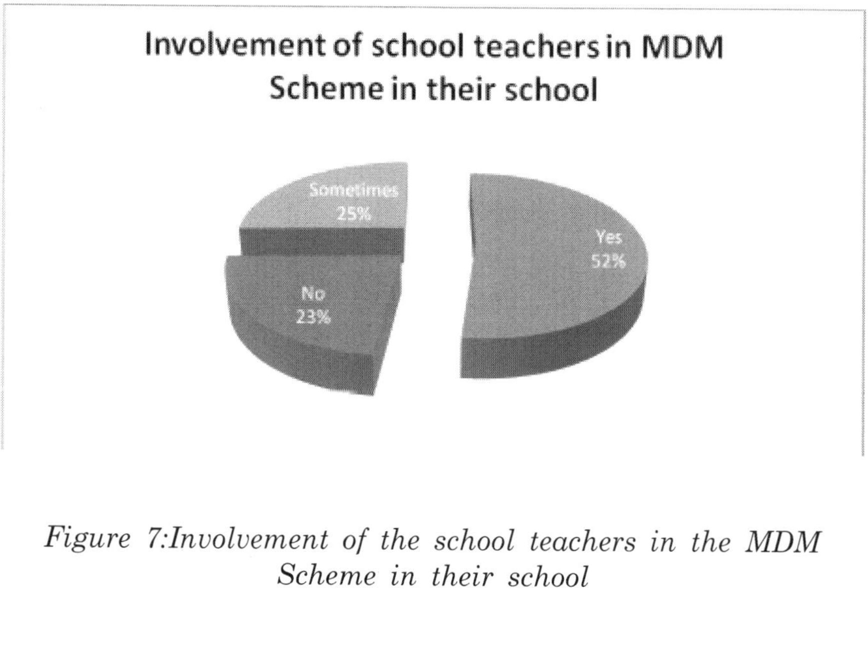

Figure 7:Involvement of the school teachers in the MDM Scheme in their school

Figure 8below indicates that very few section of the teachers believe that MDM Scheme disrupts teaching anyway. 86% teachers believe that MDM Scheme does not disrupt teaching.

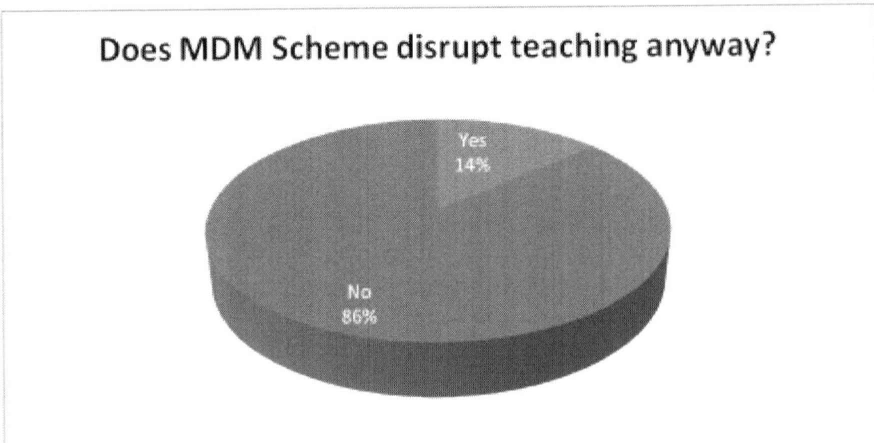

Figure 8: Do you feel that the MDM Scheme disrupts teaching anyway? – Responses by the teachers

A study by Sigma Research and Consulting Pvt. Ltd (2014) concluded that enrolment and attendance have increased significantly after the introduction of the MDM Scheme in the schools. Government officials also agreed that the MDM Scheme had a positive effect on attendance and enrolment. A study by Kusuma Trust (2012) also concludes that the MDM Scheme certainly had positive impact on the factors of attendance, enrolment, retention, socialization and health of the children. If the mid-day meal is implemented effectively and is supported with other facilities like the quality of education, proper sanitation facilities, free books and uniforms, then it can further harness the potential of the programme by increasing enrolment, retention and attendance.

This research project also tried to find out the impact of providing mid-day meals in enrolment of students in the schools.

Effect on students' enrolment due to introduction of MDM Scheme

Figure 9 below concludes that approximately 69% teachers believe that there is increase in enrollment due to introduction of mid-day meals.

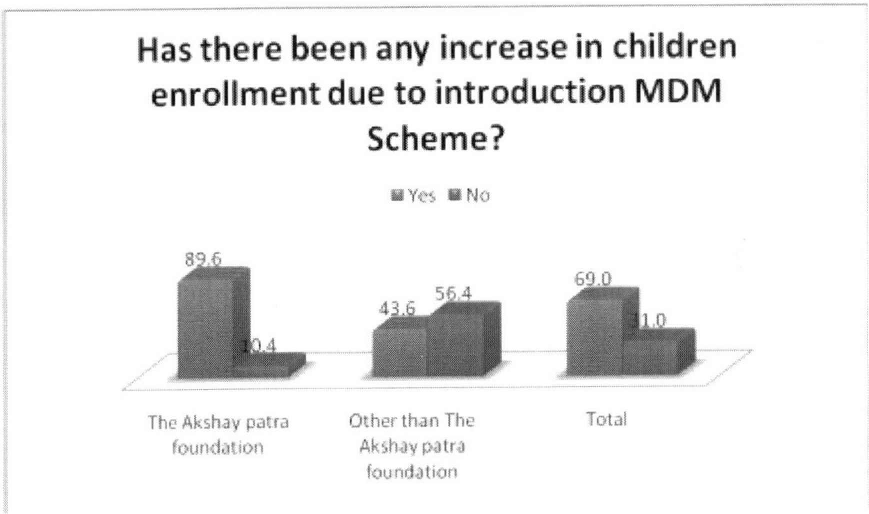

Figure 9: Has there been an increase in children enrolment due to implementation of mid-day meals?

Figure 9 also indicates the impact in schools where the Akshaya Patra Foundation serves is much higher than other schools where the Akshaya Patra Foundation does not serve.

Table 4 provides the cross tabulation between questions – **a) who provides you mid-day meals in your school?** And, **b) has there been any increase in children enrollment due to introduction of mid-day meals?**

Table 4 indicates that out of 48 teachers who are associated with the schools where the Akshaya Patra Foundation serves, only 5 teachers say that there is no increase in the enrollment of students. Whereas out of 39 teachers, who are associated with schools where the Akshaya Patra Foundation does not serve, 22 teachers say that there is no increase in the enrollment.

For deriving the statistical evidence chi-square test was carried out between said questions.

Table 4 Crosstab

		Who provides MDM in your school?		
		The Akshaya Patra Foundation	Other than the Akshaya Patra Foundation	Total
Has there been any increase in children enrollment due to introduction of MDM?	Yes	43	17	60
	No	5	22	27
Total		48	39	87

Null Hypothesis suggests that there is no statistically significant association between the two variables, namely, **"enrollment of students due to having started MDM"**, and **"serving of MDM by the Akshaya Patra Foundation."**

Table 5 provides the details of Chi-SquareTest.Pearson Chi-Square Test result value 21.267 and df 1 appear to reject the Null Hypothesis and conclude that there is statistically significant association between enrollment due to having started MDM and serving MDM by the Akshaya Patra Foundation. Fisher's Exact Test also indicates statistical significance in the line of Chi-SquareTest.

This helps us conclude that teachers who belong to the schools where the Akshaya Patra Foundation serves has more positive perception regarding an increase in enrollment of students due to MDM as compared to teachers who belong to the schools which are not served by the Akshaya Patra Foundation. The fact that there is higher enrollment of students when mid-day meals are provided is in line with the previous studies, but it also concludes that schools in which mid-day meals are served by the Akshaya Patra Foundation have comparatively greater number of enrollments.

Table 5 Chi-Square Tests

	Value	df	Asymp. Sig. (2-sided)	Exact Sig. (2-sided)	Exact Sig. (1-sided)
Pearson Chi-Square	21.267[a]	1	.000		
Continuity Correction[b]	19.172	1	.000		
Likelihood Ratio	22.271	1	.000		
Fisher's Exact Test				.000	.000
Linear-by-Linear Association	21.022	1	.000		
N of Valid Cases	87				
a. 0 cells (0.0%) have expected count less than 5. The minimum expected count is 12.10.					
b. Computed only for a 2x2 table					

Effect on Drop-out rates among students after introduction of MDM Scheme

Figure 10 below concludes that approximately 72.4% teachers believe that there isdecrease in dropout rate among the children after the introduction of MDM.

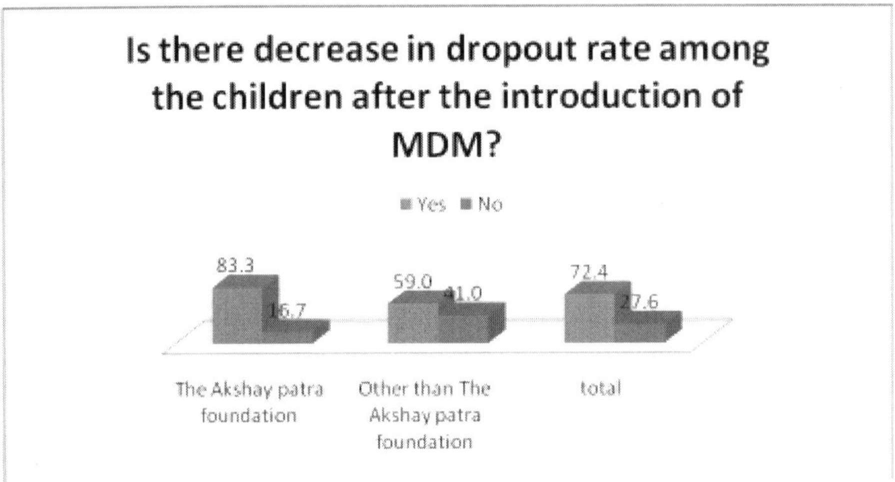

Figure 10: How would you rate the interest level of children in studies after the MDM has been started?

Figure 10 also indicates that more number of teachers of schools where the Akshaya Patra Foundation serves believe that there is decrease in the dropout ratio as compared to the number teachers of schools where the Akshaya Patra Foundation does not serve.

Table 6 provides the cross tabulation between questions – **(a)who provides you MDM in your school?** And,**(b) is there a decrease in dropout rate among the children after the introduction of MDM?**

Table 6 indicates that out of 48 teachers who belong to the schools where the Akshaya Patra Foundation serves, only 8 teachers responded saying no, there is no decrease in dropout rate among the children after the introduction of MDM. Whereas out of 39 teachers who belong to the schools where the Akshaya Patra Foundation does not serve, a higher number of 16 teachers say no, there is no decrease in dropout rate among the children after the introduction of MDM.

For deriving the statistical evidence chi-square test was carried out between said questions.

Table 6 Crosstab

		Who provides you MDM in your school?		Total
		The Akshaya Patra Foundation	Other than the Akshaya Patra Foundation	
Is there decrease in dropout rate among the children after the introduction of MDM?	Yes	40	23	63
	No	8	16	24
Total		48	39	87

Null Hypothesis suggests that there is no statistically significant association between the two variables, namely, **"dropout rate among the children after the introduction of mid-day meals"**and **"serving mid-day meals by the Akshaya Patra Foundation."**

Table 7 provides the details of Chi-SquareTest. Pearson Chi-Square Test result value 6.391 and df 1 with the p value of 0.01 clearly appear to reject the Null Hypothesis and conclude that there is statistically significant association between dropout rate among the students after the introduction of mid-day meals and serving MDM by the Akshaya Patra Foundation. Fisher's Exact

Test also indicates statistical significance in the line of Chi-Square Test.

This helps us conclude that there is a greater decrease in drop-out rates after mid-day meals have been started among students in schools in which the mid-day meals are provided by the Akshaya Patra Foundation as compared to the schools in which mid-day meals are not provided by the Akshaya Patra Foundation. The fact that there is a decrease in drop-out rates among the students because of mid-day meals is in line with the previous studies, but it also concludes that there is greater decrease in drop-out rates in schools in which mid-day meals are provided by the Akshaya Patra Foundation.

Table 7 Chi-Square Tests

	Value	df	Asymp. Sig. (2-sided)	Exact Sig. (2-sided)	Exact Sig. (1-sided)
Pearson Chi-Square	6.391[a]	1	.011		
Continuity Correction[b]	5.230	1	.022		
Likelihood Ratio	6.430	1	.011		
Fisher's Exact Test				.016	.011
Linear-by-Linear Association	6.318	1	.012		
a. 0 cells (0.0%) have expected count less than 5. The minimum expected count is 10.76.					
b. Computed only for a 2x2 table					

Effect on interest level in studies among students after introduction of MDM Scheme

Figure 11 below helps us conclude that approximately 56.3% teachers believe that interest level of students increased after the MDM Scheme has been introduced, whereas 29.9% and 13.8% teachers believed that interest level of students remain same as before and has gone down, respectively.

Figure 11 also helps us conclude that approximately 83.3% teachers of schools where the Akshaya Patra Foundation serves believe that interest level of students increased after the MDM started whereas 16.7% teachers believed that interest level of students remainsthe same as before. It is also observed that approximately 23.1% teachers of schools where the Akshaya Patra Foundation does not serve believe that interest level of students increased after the MDM started whereasa higher number of teachers, 46.2% and 30.8%, believed that interest level of students remains the same as before and has gone down, respectively.

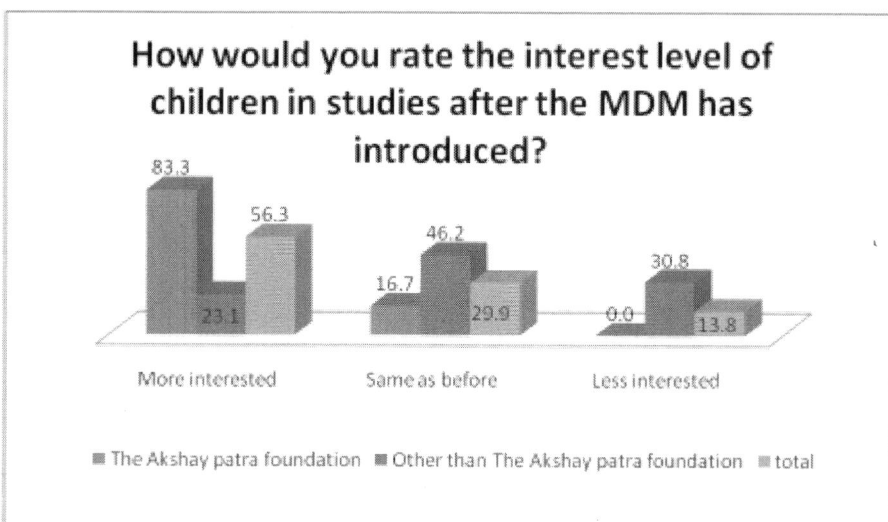

Figure 11:Effect on the interest level of children in studies after the MDM has been introduced.

Table 8 below provides the cross tabulation between questions– **(a) who provides you MDM in your school?**And, **(b) how would you rate the interest level of children in studies after the MDM has started?**

Table 8 indicates that out of 48 teachers who belong to the schools where the Akshaya Patra Foundation serves, only 8 teachers say interest level remainsthe same as before while no teachers said that interest level has gone down. Whereas out of 39 teachers whobelong to the schools where the Akshaya Patra Foundation does not serve, 18 teachers say interest level remainsthe same as before and 12 teachers said that interest level has gone down.

For deriving the statistical evidence chi-square test was carried out between said questions.

Table 8 Crosstab

		Who provides you MDM in your school?		Total
		The Akshaya Patra Foundation	Other than the Akshaya Patra Foundation	
How would you rate the interest level of children in studies after the MDM has started?	More interested	40	9	49
	Same as before	8	18	26
	Less interested	0	12	12
Total		48	39	87

Null hypothesis suggests that there is no statistically significant association between the two variables, namely, **"interest level of children in studies after the introduction of mid-day meals"** and MDM has started and **"serving mid-day meals by the Akshaya Patra Foundation."**

Table 9 provides the details of Chi-Square Test. Pearson Chi-Square Test result value 34.901 and df 2 with the p value of 0.00 clearly appear to reject the Null Hypothesis and conclude that there is statistically significant association between interest level of children in studies after the introduction of mid-day meals and serving MDM by the Akshaya Patra Foundation.

Chi-SquareTest helps us conclude that more number of teachers who belong to the schools in which mid-day meals are provided by the Akshaya Patra Foundation believe that interest level of children has gone up as compared to the teachers from schools which are not served by the Akshaya Patra Foundation.

Table 9 Chi-Square Tests

	Value	df	Asymp. Sig. (2-sided)
Pearson Chi-Square	34.901[a]	2	.000
Likelihood Ratio	40.840	2	.000
Linear-by-Linear Association	33.873	1	.000
N of Valid Cases	87		
a. 0 cells (0.0%) have expected count less than 5. The minimum expected count is 5.38.			

Effect on an overall improvement in health among students after introduction of MDM Scheme

Figure 12helps us conclude that approximately 67.8% teachers believe there is health improvement after MDM having started whereas 32.2% teachers believed that there is no health improvement after having MDM started.

Figure 12 also helps us conclude that approximately 75.0% teachers of schools where the Akshaya Patra Foundation serves believe that there is health improvement after having started MDM whereas 25.0% teachers believed that there is no health improvement after having started MDM. It is also observed that approximately 59.0% teachers of schools where the Akshaya Patra Foundation does not serve believe that there is health improvement after having MDM started whereas 41.0% teachers believed that there is no health improvement after having started MDM.

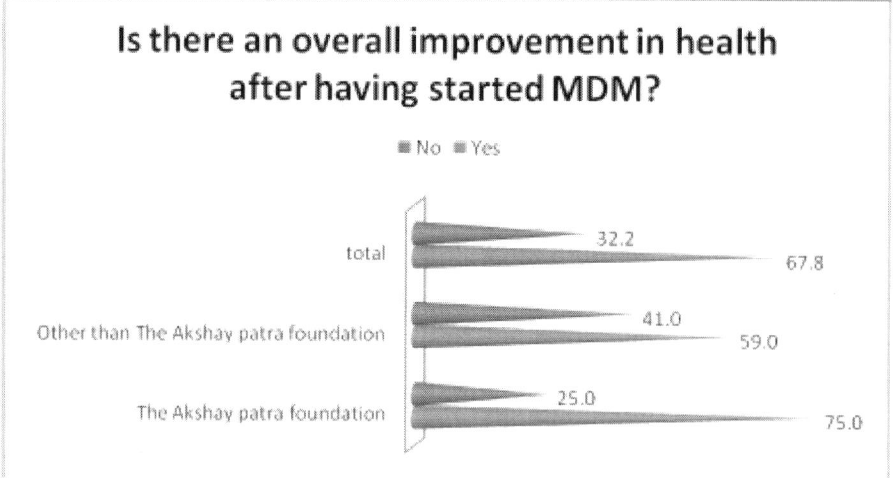

Figure 12:Health improvement in the child after having access to mid-day meals

Table 10below provides the cross tabulation between questions – **(a) who provides you mid-day meals in your school?**and, **(b) is there an overall improvement in health after having started mid-day meals?**

Table 10 indicates that out of 48 teachers who belong to the schools where the Akshaya Patra Foundation serves, only 12 teachers say there is no health improvement after having started MDM whereas out of 39 teachers who belong to the schools where the Akshaya Patra Foundation does not serve, 16 teachers say there is no health improvement after having started MDM.

For deriving the statistical evidence chi-square test was carried out between said questions.

Table 10 Crosstab

		Who provides you MDM in your school?		Total
		The Akshaya Patra Foundation	Other than the Akshaya Patra Foundation	
Is there anoverall improvement in health after having started MDM?	Yes	36	23	59
	No	12	16	28
Total		48	39	87

Null hypothesis suggests that there is no statistically significant association between the two variables, namely, **"overall improvement in health after the introduction of mid-day meals"** and **"serving mid-day meals by the Akshaya Patra Foundation."**

Table 11 provides the details of Chi-SquareTest. Pearson Chi-Square Test result value 2.532 and df 1 with the p value of 0.112 fail to reject the Null Hypothesis and conclude that there is no statistically significant association between **"overall improvement in health afterthe introduction of mid-day meals"** and **"serving mid-day meals by the Akshaya Patra Foundation."**

Table 11 Chi-Square Tests

	Value	df	Asymp. Sig. (2-sided)	Exact Sig. (2-sided)	Exact Sig. (1-sided)
Pearson Chi-Square	2.532[a]	1	.112		
Continuity Correction[b]	1.851	1	.174		
Likelihood Ratio	2.529	1	.112		
Fisher's Exact Test				.166	.087
Linear-by-Linear Association	2.503	1	.114		
N of Valid Cases	87				
a. 0 cells (0.0%) have expected count less than 5. The minimum expected count is 12.55.					
b. Computed only for a 2x2 table					

Overall perception and opinion of the teachers regarding various aspects of the MDM such as taste, quantity, quality, variety, punctuality, freshness, cleanliness and hygiene, nutritional level and aroma etc. was measured through their response to a set of 16 statements on a five-point scale where 1 means "strongly disagree" and 5 means "strongly agree". (Refer to Table 12)

Table 12 Perception and opinion regarding MDM

Statements	Total		The Akshaya Patra Foundation		Other than the Akshaya Patra Foundation	
	Mean	SD	Mean	SD	Mean	SD
I believe that the taste of food is good	3.80	0.86	4.27	0.61	3.23	0.78
The food is provided in sufficient in quantity	3.75	0.78	4.19	0.57	3.21	0.66
The menu varies every day	3.91	0.71	4.29	0.62	3.44	0.50
The food is provided on time	3.71	0.90	4.00	0.88	3.36	0.81
The foods provided is fresh	3.71	0.79	4.10	0.52	3.23	0.81
The distribution of food is under the supervision of teachers and helpers	3.85	0.72	3.90	0.81	3.79	0.61
The utensils and serving plates are well sanitized.	3.95	0.66	4.27	0.45	3.56	0.68

There is consistency and regularity in delivery of mid-daymeals	3.74	0.69	4.08	0.50	3.31	0.66
The teachers and helpers emphasize to maintain good personal hygiene	3.78	0.88	3.96	1.07	3.56	0.50
I believe that consistency of mid-day meals improves performance	3.79	0.59	3.98	0.60	3.56	0.50
I believe that consistency of mid-day meals improves learning	3.85	0.66	4.08	0.68	3.56	0.50
I believe that mid-day meals help to become more socialized by eating in a group	3.55	0.90	3.79	0.92	3.26	0.79
I believe that consistency of mid-day meals improves overall health.	3.61	0.67	3.73	0.76	3.46	0.51
Mid-day meals provide nutritious food	3.55	0.59	3.63	0.64	3.46	0.51

Mid-day meals provide aromatic food which induces the urge to eat	3.11	1.11	3.27	1.22	2.92	0.96
I believe that eating mid-day meals is delightful and satisfactory experience for students	3.24	1.11	3.73	1.01	2.64	0.93

Table 12 helps us conclude that perception and opinion scores regarding MDM of teachers of schools where the Akshaya Patra Foundation serves is higher as compared to the teachers of schools where the Akshaya Patra Foundation does not serve. Overall teachers believe that MDM hasa positive and notable effect on the students and these effects are more positive and notable in schools whichare served by the Akshaya Patra Foundation.

Response of Students

A total of 486 students were surveyed in this project. Out of them, 267 students belong to schools where the Akshaya Patra Foundation provides MDM and remaining 219 students belong to schools where MDM is served by agencies or organizations other than the Akshaya Patra Foundation.

Figure 13 indicates that majority of the students do not eat anything in the morning. 60% students do not take breakfast before coming to school whereas 20% students take breakfast regularly and 20% students take breakfast occasionally.

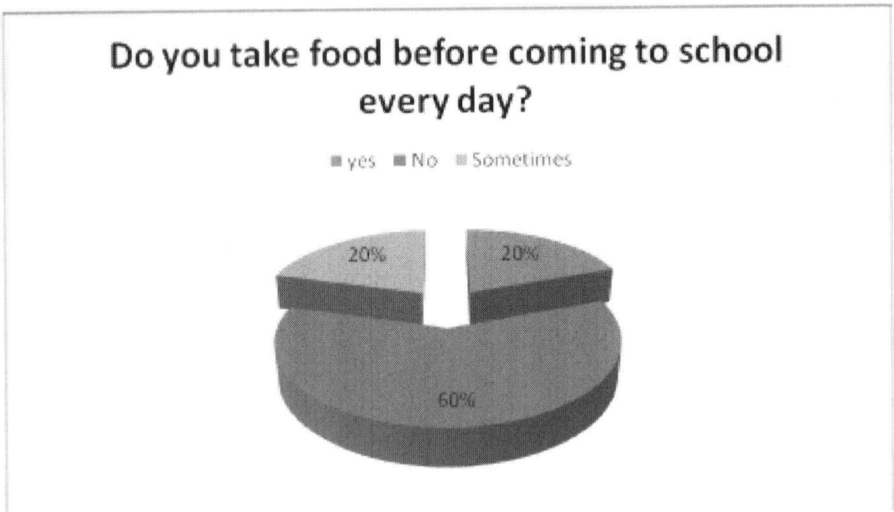

Figure 13: Do you take food before coming to school every day?– Responses by students

Figure 14 indicates that approximately 60% students do not eat anything before coming to school; of the remaining 40% who take breakfast in the morning, 15% students take rice, followed by other light food (11.3%), roti/chapatti (9.9%) and curry (4.1%).

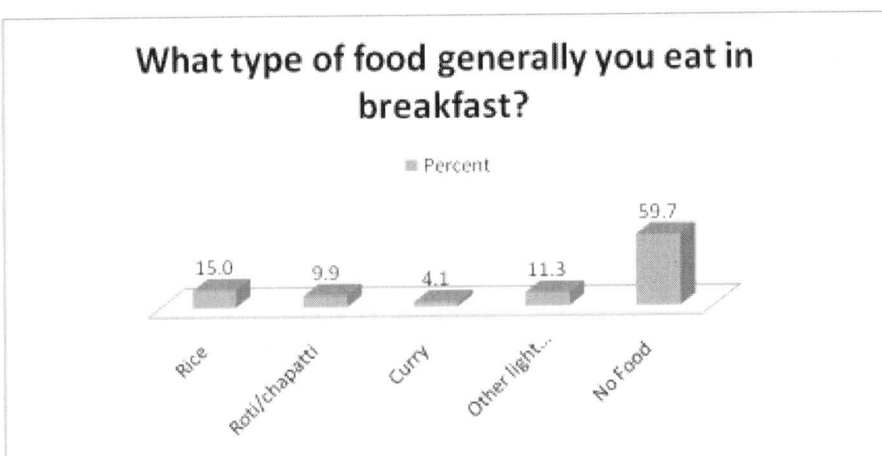

Figure 14: What type of food do you generally eat in breakfast?– Responses by students

Figure 15 indicates that MDM is one the most important factors which attract the students towards the school. 30.2% students said that they like MDM most about their school, followed by study (30%), friends and school environment (24.9%) and teachers (14.8).

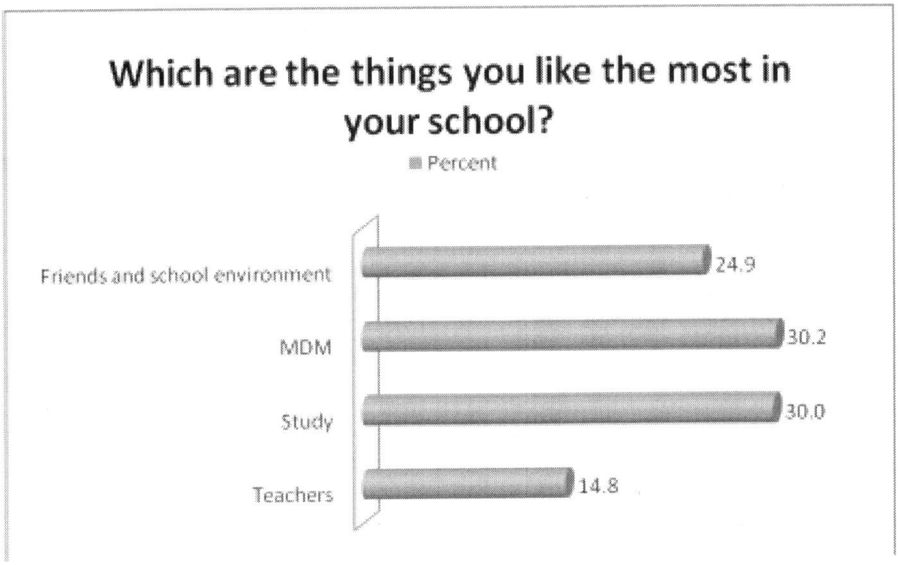

Figure 15: Which are the things you like the most in your school? – Responses by students

Overall perception and opinion of students regarding various aspects of MDM

Overall perception and opinion of the students regarding various aspects of the MDM such as taste, quantity, quality, variety, punctuality, freshness, cleanliness and hygiene, nutritional level and aroma etc. was measured through their response to a set of 16 statements on a five-point scale where 1 means "strongly disagree" and 5 means "strongly agree".

Two independent T tests were applied to find out the mean score of these 16 perceptual statements of the Akshaya Patra

Foundation serving schools and the other schools. (Refer to Table 13)

Table 13 Independent Samples Test

	t-test for Equality of Means		
	t	df	Sig. (2-tailed)
I believe that the taste of food is good	16.43	484	.000
The food is provided in sufficient in quantity	17.784	484	.000
The menu varies every day	20.805	484	.000
The food is provided on time	11.405	484	.000
The foods provided is fresh	15.459	484	.000
The distribution of food is under the supervision of teachers and helpers	7.964	484	.000
The utensils and serving plates are well sanitized	15.313	484	.000
There is consistency and regularity in delivery of mid-day meals	20.167	484	.000
The teachers and helpers emphasize to maintain good personal hygiene	6.373	484	.000
I believe that consistency of mid-day meals improves performance	16.087	484	.000

I believe that consistency of mid-day meals improves learning	13.241	484	.000
I believe that mid-day meals help to become more socialized by eating in a group	11.391	484	.000
I believe that consistency of mid-day meals improves overall health.	6.539	484	.000
Mid-day meals provide nutritious food	12.471	484	.000
Mid-day meals provide aromatic food which induces the urge to eat	6.393	484	.000
I believe that eating mid-day meals is delightful and satisfactory experience for students	11.143	484	.000

Table 13 indicates that all the t test results are statistically significant as the P value of all the statements are 0.000 which is less than the significant level, which helps us conclude that there is significant difference in the mean score of both groups.

Table 14 below provides the mean score of all the 16 statements for schools where the Akshaya Patra Foundation serves and for schools where the Akshaya Patra Foundation does not serve. Table 14 clearly indicates that the Akshaya Patra Foundation is performing better in all aspects of the MDM as compared to the others. All the factors namely taste, quantity, quality, variety, punctuality, freshness, proper distribution, cleanliness, consistency, hygiene, nutrition level and aroma etc. have the ahigher mean as compared to the others.

Table 14 Group Statistics

Who provides you MDM in your school?		N	Mean	Std. Deviation
The taste of food is good	The Akshaya Patra Foundation	267	4.27	0.75
	Other than the Akshaya Patra Foundation	219	3.22	0.63
The food is provided in sufficient quantity	The Akshaya Patra Foundation	267	4.19	0.72
	Other than the Akshaya Patra Foundation	219	3.01	0.73
The menu varies every day	The Akshaya Patra Foundation	267	4.45	0.66
	Other than the Akshaya Patra Foundation	219	3.22	0.63
The food is provided on time	The Akshaya Patra Foundation	267	4.00	0.85

	Other than the Akshaya Patra Foundation	219	3.11	0.88
The food provided is fresh	The Akshaya Patra Foundation	267	4.18	0.58
	Other than the Akshaya Patra Foundation	219	3.22	0.79
The distribution of food is under the supervision of teachers and helpers	The Akshaya Patra Foundation	267	4.09	0.67
	Other than the Akshaya Patra Foundation	219	3.55	0.83
The utensils and serving plates are well sanitized	The Akshaya Patra Foundation	267	4.37	0.48
	Other than the Akshaya Patra Foundation	219	3.44	0.83
There is consistency and regularity in delivery of mid-day meals	The Akshaya Patra Foundation	267	4.18	0.39
	Other than the Akshaya Patra Foundation	219	3.00	0.85

The teachers and helpers emphasize to maintain good personal hygiene	The Akshaya Patra Foundation	267	4.09	1.16
	Other than the Akshaya Patra Foundation	219	3.55	0.50
Consistency of mid-day meals improves performance	The Akshaya Patra Foundation	267	4.09	0.67
	Other than the Akshaya Patra Foundation	219	3.01	0.82
Consistency of mid-day meals improves learning	The Akshaya Patra Foundation	267	4.10	0.67
	Other than the Akshaya Patra Foundation	219	3.22	0.78
Mid-day meals help to become more socialized by eating in a group	The Akshaya Patra Foundation	267	4.01	0.95
	Other than the Akshaya Patra Foundation	219	3.05	0.87
Consistency of mid-day meals improves overall health.	The Akshaya Patra Foundation	267	3.82	0.72

	Other than the Akshaya Patra Foundation	219	3.44	0.50
Mid-day meals provide nutritious food	The Akshaya Patra Foundation	267	4.00	0.74
	Other than the Akshaya Patra Foundation	219	3.22	0.63
Mid-day meals provide aromatic food which induces the urge to eat	The Akshaya Patra Foundation	267	3.64	1.23
	Other than the Akshaya Patra Foundation	219	3.00	0.94
Eating mid-day meals is delightful and satisfactory experience	The Akshaya Patra Foundation	267	4.00	0.95
	Other than the Akshaya Patra Foundation	219	3.01	1.00

Overall this research project concludes that the Akshaya Patra Foundation has very satisfactory performance in Gujarat in schools where they provide mid-day meals. MDM Scheme with the help of the Akshaya Patra Foundation has a significant impact on the enrollment level, decrease in the dropout rates besides greater involvement in the studies. Apart from that they are serving mid-day meals with appropriate standards of quality.

Need and prospects of the Akshaya Patra Foundation in interior Gujarat

Akshaya Patra scheme is working only in urban areasor the main cities of the state. In Gujarat only four cities are still covered, while one has just been opened in Kalol. However, real need of this scheme is for the rural sections of the country which are yet not served by them. In Gujarat, Dang and Tapi districts have the highest proportion of severely underweight children and Narmada, Tapi, Chhota Udepur and Dang have the highest percentage of total underweight. Schools from these districts are also included for the study; 39 teachers and 219 students were selected and interviewed regarding the need of the Akshaya Patra Foundation.

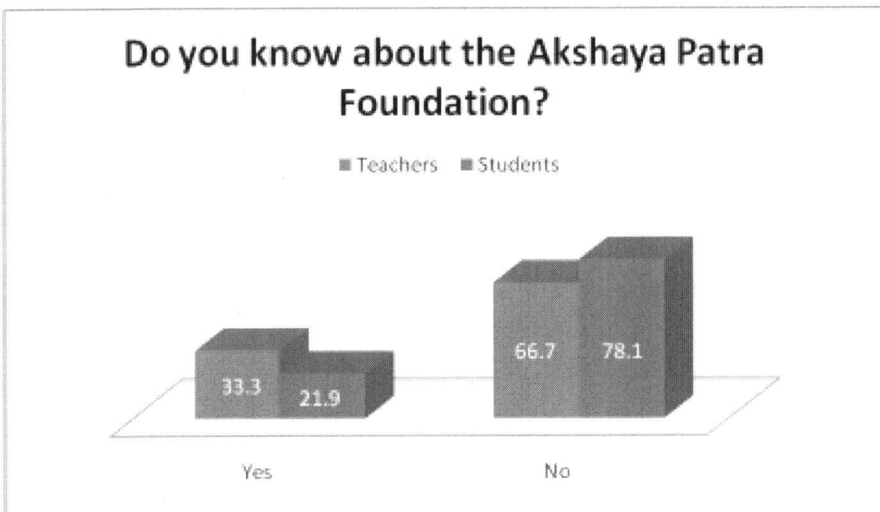

Figure 16: Do you know about the Akshaya Patra Foundation? – Responses by students and teachers

As the above Figure 16 indicates, awareness of the Akshaya Patra Foundation is very low in the interior parts of Gujarat among students (78.1%) as well as teachers (66.7%).

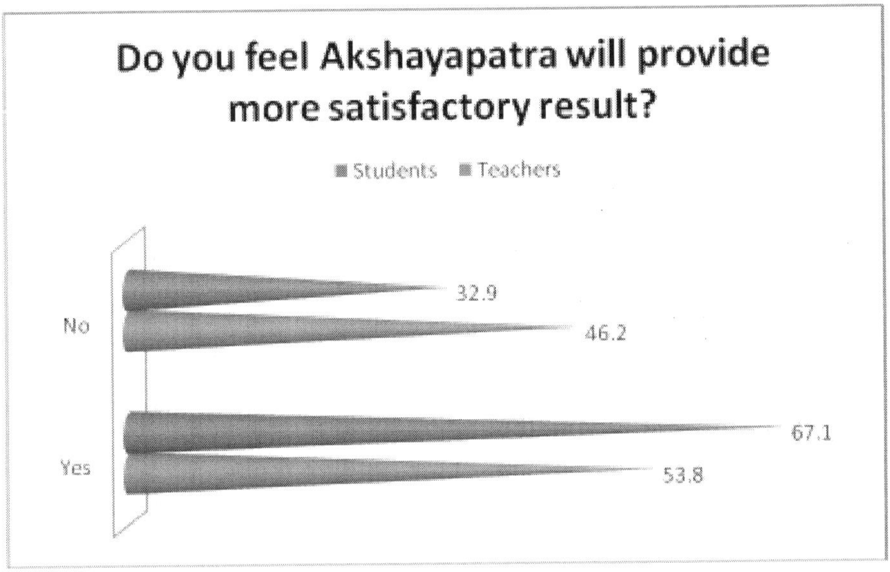

Figure 17: Do you feel Akshaya Patrainitiative will provide more satisfactory result? –responses by students and teachers

Information regarding the Akshaya Patra Foundation was given to students and teachers and then subsequently queried whether involving Akshaya Patra Foundation would provide more satisfactory result? As Figure 17 indicates, 53.8% teachers and 67.1% students believed in affirmative.

Figure 18 indicates that 64.1% teachers and 78.1% students said that they would like to avail services of Akshaya Patra Foundation in their school.

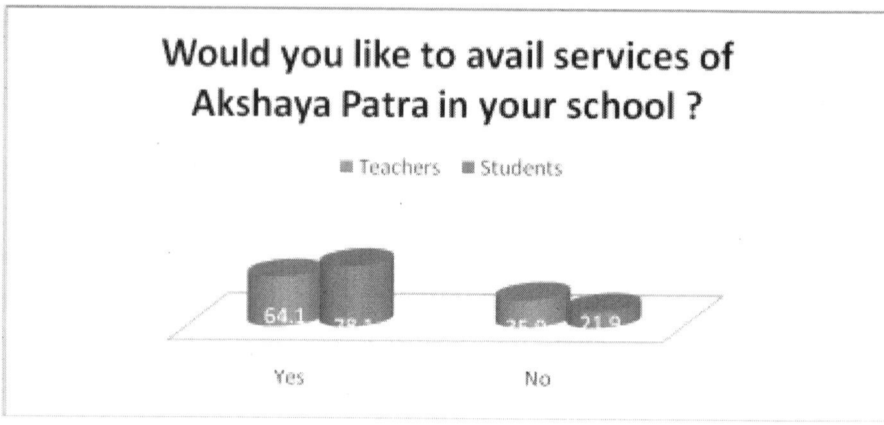

Figure 18: Would you like to avail services of Akshaya Patra in your school? – Responses by students and teachers

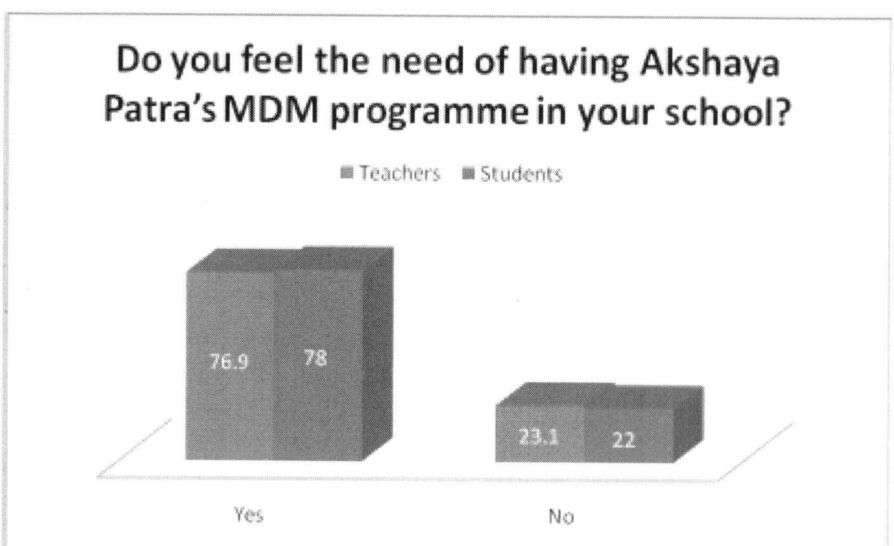

Figure 19: Do you feel the need of having of Akshaya Patra's MDM Scheme in your school?– Responses by students and teachers

Figure 19 indicates that approximately 78% students and 76.9% teachers feel that there is a need of Akshaya Patra Foundation in their school.

5

FINDINGS AND CONCLUSIONS OF THE RESEARCH PROJECT

Findings of the Research Project

- The Akshaya Patra Foundation reaches out to over 1.7 million children in 14,173 schools, across 12 states in India. The mid-day meal in Gujarat is served through centralized kitchens.
- The Vadodara kitchen was established first in 2009, followed by Surat in 2012, Ahmedabad in 2014, Bhavnagar in 2017 and most recently by Kalol. The five kitchens together feed 4,07,452 children in 1,621 schools every day in Gujarat
- Majority of the teachers, around 52%, said yes, they are involved in MDM whereas 25% teachers said they are involved only sometimes in the MDM at school level.
- 86% teachers believe that MDM does not disrupt the teaching.
- This research project finds that approximately 69% teachers believe that there is increase in enrolment due to MDM. There is statistically significant association between enrolment due to MDM Scheme and serving mid-day meals the Akshaya Patra Foundation. Perception of teachers who belong to schools where the Akshaya Patra Foundation is active is more positive regarding higher enrolment of

students due to MDM Scheme as compared to teachers belonging to schools where the Akshaya Patra Foundation does not serve.

- This research project also finds that 72.4% teachers believe that there is decrease in dropout rate among the children after the introduction of MDM Scheme. There is statistically significant association between decrease in dropout rate among the children after the introduction of MDM Scheme and mid-day meals served by the Akshaya Patra Foundation. More number of teachers of schools where the Akshaya Patra Foundation serves believe that there is decrease in the dropout ratio as compared to teachers who belong to the schools where the Akshaya Patra Foundation does not serve.
- The fact that there is a decrease in dropout rate among the students because of introduction of mid-day meals is in line with the previous studies, but it also concludes that in schools served by the Akshaya Patra Foundation, this decrease is have comparatively higher.
- This research project reveals that 56.3% teachers believe that interest level of students increased after the MDM Scheme has been introduced, whereas 29.9% and 13.8% teachers believed that interest level of students remained same as before and hagone down, respectively. Of the schools in which the Akshaya Patra Foundation serves, 83.3% teachers believe that interest level of students has gone up after the MDM Scheme has been introduced, whereasonly 16.7% teachers believed that interest level of students remainsthe same as before.
- It is also observed that of schools where the Akshaya Patra Foundation does not serve, 23.1% teachers believe that interest level of students has gone up after the MDM Scheme has been introduced, whereas 46.2% and 30.8% teachers believed that interest level of students remain same as before and has gone down, respectively.
- There is statistically significant association between an

increase in interest level of children in studies after the MDM Scheme has been introduced and servingmid-day meals by the Akshaya Patra Foundation. It further concludes that teachers who belong to the schools where the Akshaya Patra Foundation serves has more positive perception regarding interest level of children in studies after the mid-day meals have been started as compared to teachers belonging to schools in which the Akshaya Patra Foundation does not serve.

- This research project also finds that 67.8% teachers believe that there is health improvement after mid-day meals have been started whereas 32.2% teachers believe that there is no health improvement. Of the schools in which mid-day meals are provided by the Akshaya Patra Foundation, 75.0% teachers of schools believe that there is health improvement after mid-day meals have been started whereas 25.0% teachers believe that there is no health improvement. Of the schools in which mid-day meals are not provided by the Akshaya Patra Foundation, 59.0% teachers believe that there is health improvement after mid-day meals have been introduced whereas 41.0% teachers believe that there is no health improvement. There is no statistically significant association between "an overall improvement in health improvement after the introduction of mid-meals"and "serving mid-day meals by the Akshaya Patra Foundation".
- Perception and opinion scores of teachers regarding an improvement in health after MDM Scheme has been introduced is higher in schools in which the Akshaya Patra Foundation serves as compared to the teachers belonging to schools where the Akshaya Patra Foundation does not serve.
- 60% students do not take breakfast before coming to school whereas 20% students take breakfast regularly and 20% students take breakfast only sometimes.
- 60% students do not eat anything before coming to school;

of the remaining 40% students who take breakfast in the morning, 15% students take rice in breakfast followed by those taking light food (11.3%), roti/chapatti (9.9%) and curry (4.1%).

- 30.2% students said that they like mid-day meals the most about their school, followed by study (30%), friends and school environment (24.9%) and teachers (14.8).
- The mean score of all the 16 statementsfor the factors namely taste, quantity, quality, variety, punctuality, freshness, proper distribution, cleanliness, consistency, hygiene, nutrition level and aroma etc. is higher for schools where the Akshaya Patra Foundation serves as compared the other schools which are not served by the Akshaya Patra Foundation.
- Awareness of the Akshaya Patra Foundation is very low in the interior part of the Gujarat. Only 33.3% teachers were aware about the Akshaya Patra Foundation while only 21.9% students were aware about the Akshaya Patra Foundation.
- 53.8% teachers believe that if the Akshaya Patra Foundation served mid-day meals in their schools then it can provide a more satisfactory result, while 67.1%students believe that if the Akshaya Patra Foundation served mid-day meals in their schools then it can provide more satisfactory result.
- 64.1% said that they would like to avail services of the Akshaya Patra in their school while 78.1% students said that they would like to avail services of Akshaya Patra in their school.
- 78% students and teachers feel that there is a need of Akshaya Patra in their school.

CONCLUSIONS OF THE RESEARCH PROJECT

This research project starts with the qualitative analysis of the data and concludes that in Gujarat, Dang and Tapi districts have the highest proportion of severely underweight children,

Narmada, Tapi, Chhota Udepur and Dang have the highest percentage of total underweight. Akshaya Patra scheme is working in main cities and urban areas only. In Gujarat there are only four main cities still covered and one recently opened in Kalol but real need of this scheme is for the rural and interior areas of the country which are yet to be covered.

This research project then measures the performance through the two questionnaires, one for the teachers and one for the students. It concludes that majority of teachers are involved in MDM directly or indirectly. It also concludes that mid-day meals have a positive effect on the enrolment, health and interest in studies by the students besides helping to contain and curb the school dropout rates. Teachers have opined that the Akshaya Patra Foundation has more significant impact on the enrolment, reduction in dropout rate, health improvement and interest level of students in studies.

Analysis of perception and opinion of the students regarding MDM Scheme helps us conclude that the Akshaya Patra Foundation has a higher score on all 16 variables namely taste, quantity, quality, variety, punctuality, freshness, proper distribution, cleanliness, consistency, hygiene, nutrition level, socialization, satisfaction and aroma etc. which indicates that the Akshaya Patra Foundation is performing well on these parameters.

It infers that in the interior areas of Gujarat awareness regarding the Akshaya Patra Foundation and its initiatives on mid-day meals is low. However, students and teachers of the interior areas of Gujarat do believe that the Akshaya Patra Foundation and mid-day meals are needed and can provide the MDM service more satisfactorily. They indicated that they would like to avail the service of the Akshaya Patra Foundation in their areas.

Challenges

- The raw materials used for preparing mid-day meal can be classified into subsidized and non-subsidized. Government-subsidized food grains such as rice and fortified *atta* form the major portion of the meal. Non-subsidized food can further be classified into two types: groceries such as *moong dal* and oil and vegetables such as tomatoes. Essentially, the Akshaya Patra Foundation deals with three types of raw materials: dry food grains - subsidized, dry food grains – non-subsidized, and green foods such as vegetables. A lot of time and cost is spent in cleaning the subsidized dry food grains such as rice and wheat.

- There are marginal differences in grocery rates due to the natural pricing variation by different suppliers.
- Production planning is a key factor for appropriate quantity of meal production every day. On a daily basis, the drivers and helpers get information, such as the number of children attending school, from the school authorities. This is considered as the real input for the next day's production. Any change in this data may cause substantial wastage of food which is critical and needs to be avoided.
- There is significant loss in the *roti*-making process due to recycling (re-feeding the remaining portion of flattened dough after cutting and removing circular *rotis*) and poor quality (undercooked or overcooked) of product.
- Any breakdown of equipment being used in the kitchen is another considerable cause of delay.
- It is also difficult to deliver food to rural areas. Roads are not paved and the infrastructure is lacking. Even if food makes it to these remote areas, kitchens to cook the food are not available in nearby vicinity.
- The issue of cooking in open spaces, rotis and rice being prepared in different places are not easy to sort out.
- There is lack of proper infrastructure in the schools. In number of schools, it is difficult to construct kitchens due to insufficiency of funds for construction and maintenance which is vital. Storage provisions are rarely available in most of the schools. There is unplanned arrangement for storage of items and in many schools these are kept in the

school office, staff room or in the classrooms. It is also noticed that meal is distributed among the children inside classrooms, *verandah* or in open spaces of the school.

Overcoming the Challenges

- Estimates for the next day's requirements are obtained by respective drivers and helpers every day at the time of delivery to individual schools. There is thus one day lag between the estimation of requirement and the actual requirement on a given day. Some variability of consumption is inevitable. It is obvious that real inputs are required before the start of food production due to certain time window associated with cooking. On an average, the cooking process takes 3-4 hours in the morning. The wastage of food due to absenteeism of children would not be more than 30% at an overall aggregate level (assuming on an average 70% attendance). There is the possibility of cutting and readjusting the expected aggregate estimate of the previous day to the real time aggregate estimate of a given day by collecting additional information from the school authorities in the first hour of school. Assuming that 40 to 60% of the food is already prepared based on the previous day's estimate the planning department can regulate the quantity of further production based on the revised estimate.
- Identification of the causes of poor quality and subsequent use of quality control practices (controlling temperature and flow of *roti* through burner, improvement in technology being used) can reduce wastage.
- Productive maintenance practices such as scheduled maintenance, preventive maintenance, and record keeping of failure of such incidents can be initiated.
- Appropriate measures in terms of additional expenditure and managerial practices can help resolve these problems to some extent.

REFERENCES

Afridi, E. (2005) "Mid-Day Meals in Two States – Comparing the Financial and Institutional Organisation of the Programme", Economic and Political Weekly, April, pp. 1528-1534.

Alim, F., Khalil, S., Mirz, I., & Khan, Z. (2012). "Impact of Mid-Day Meal Scheme on the Nutritional Status and Academic Achievement of School Children in Aligarh City". Indian Journal of Science Research, Vol. 30, No. 2 pp.85-95.

Anima, R. and Sharma, N.K. (2008). "An Empirical Study of the Mid-Day Meal Programme in Khurda, Orissa", Economic and Political Weekly, Vol.43, No.25, pp. 46-55.

Babar NF et al.(2010), "Impact of Socioeconomic Factors On Nutritional Status In Primary School Children" J Ayub Medical College, Abbottabad 2010;22(4):15-18.

Behrman, J. R. (1996),The Impact of Health and Nutrition on Education. World Bank Research Observer, 11(1), pp. 23-37.

Bellary A.,"Assessment of Nutritional Profile of Beneficiaries of Akshara Dasoha Programme and Implementation Status in Hubli City", Ph.D. Dissertation, University of Agricultural Sciences, 2009.

Bhargav S and Bhargav A, An Evaluative Study of Opinion and Awareness of Primary School Teachers Towards Implementation of Mid-Day Meal Program, EXCEL International Journal of Multidisciplinary Management Studies, 2011;1(1):21-30.

Deodhar S, Mahandiratta S, Ramani K, et al.Mid-Day Meal

Scheme: Understanding Critical Issues with Reference to Ahmedabad City, (No. 2007-03, p. 03) Working Paper, (2007).

Directorate of Public Instruction, Raipur, Chhatisgarh. Aide et Action - South Asia. Evaluation of the On-going Mid-Day Meal Programme in Primary Schools of Chhattisgarh State, 2008.

G. Srihari et al.(2007), "Nutritional Status of Affluent Indian School Children: What and How Much Do We Know?" Indian Paediatrics 2007;44(17):204-213.

Garvita Jain, Dr.(Smt) S.K.Bharadwaj, Dr.(Smt) Abhaya R. Joglekar (2012), "To study the prevalence of overweight and obesity among school children (13-17yrs) in relation to their socio-economic status and eating habits" International Journal of Scientific and Research Publications 2012;2(6):1-4.

Govt. of India, Ministry of Information & Broadcasting (2008). "India 2008 – A Reference Annual". New Delhi: Ministry of Information and Broadcasting.

Govt. of India. (2008). MDM - PAB to Consider and Approve WAP&B 2008-09 (Appraisal Note: Orissa). New Delhi: Government of India.

Govt. of Odisha, Deptt. of School Mass Education (2013). Report on MDM (2013). Bhubaneswar: Department of School and Mass Education.

Govt. of Odisha. Deptt. of School & Mass Education (2013). Contingency Plan For Management of Mid-Day Meal Scheme (2013).

Grantham-McGregor, S. (1995) A Review of the Studies of the Effect of Severe Malnutrition on Mental Development. The Journal of Nutrition, 125(8) pp.2233-2238.

Hall A, Tran T, Katherine F, et al. An Evaluation of the Impact of a School Nutrition Programme in Vietnam. Public Health Nutrition, 2007, 10(8): 819-826.

Hamid Y and Hamid A. Mid-DayMeal Scheme and Growth of Primary Education: A Case Study of District Anantnag in

Jammu and Kashmir. Bangladesh e-Journal of Sociology, 2012, 9(1): 80-88.

Kapur, A. and Chowdhury, A. (2012). "Mid-Day Meal Scheme. GOI, 2012-13," Budget Briefs Mid-Day Meal, Vol.4, Issue 4, New Delhi: Accountability Initiative.

Khera, R. (2006) "Mid-Day Meals in Primary Schools". Economic and Political Weekly, Vol. 41, No.46.

Mid-Day Meal Annual Work Plan & Budget 2013-14. Commissionerate of Mid-Day Meal, Gujarat.http://mdm.nic.in/ Files/PAB/PAB2013- 14/Gujarat/Gujarat_State_Plan.pdf.

Mishra, S.N. (2003). "Nutritional Support to Primary Education (Mid-Day Meal Programme) in Orissa, Its Impact on Enrolment, Attendance, Retention, and Dropouts Among Primary School Going Children". In Vision 2020 – An Agenda for School and Mass Education. Bhubaneswar:Government of Orissa, pp.362-374.

Nambiyar S, Pande G and Solanki J. Innovation in Delivery of Mid-Day Meal Scheme Through Private Public Partnership. NAPSIPAG 7th International Conference, 2010.

One World Foundation India (OWFI), Governance Knowledge Centre. Akshaya Patra Mid-Day Meal Programme. A Case Study, 2012: 1-15.

ORG Centre for Social Research. Impact assessment of the Akshaya Patra Foundation (TAPF) Mid-Day meal programme, Jaipur, 2006.

Panda, B.K. (2010). "Achieving Universal Primary Education- Mid-Day Meal Programme in Residential Schools for the Scheduled Tribes in Chhattisgarh", Journal of Indian Education, Vol.34, No.4, pp. 59-74.

Pandey S, Bhaskaran A, Agashe S, Vaidya R (2014). "A cross-sectional study of childhood and adolescent obesity in affluent school children from western suburb of Mumbai" 2001-2002 & 2013-2014. J ObesMetab Res 2014;1:7-13.

Pathania, A. and Pathania, K. (2006). Primary Education and Mid-Day Meal Scheme-Results, Challenges and Recommendations. New Delhi: Deep & Deep Publications Pvt. Ltd.

Porter C, Singh A and Sinha A. The Impact of the Mid-Day Meal Scheme on Nutrition and Learning. Young Lives Policy Brief, 2010.

Samson M, Noronha C and AnuradhaD., "Towards more benefits from Delhi's Mid-Day Meal Scheme." New Delhi: CORD Collaborative Research and Dissemination, 2007.

Saxena, R.R. and Mittal, S.C. (1985). "Impact of Mid-Day Programme on Enrolment and Retention at the Primary Stage". Project Report. New Delhi: NCERT.

Sharma S, Passi S, Thomas S, et al. Evaluation of Mid-Day Meal Programme in MCD schools. Study supported by Municipal Corporation of Delhi, Nutrition Foundation of India, Scientific Report 18, 2006.

Sikligar, P.C. (2011). Mid-Day Meal Scheme and School Education: Planning, Implementation and Effectiveness. New Delhi: Concept Publishing Company Pvt. Ltd.

Singh, A.; Park, A. and Dercon, S. (2012). "School Meals as a Safety Net: An Evaluation of the Mid- Day Meal Scheme in India," Working Paper No. 75. Oxford: University of Oxford.

Srinivas, K. A Study of Best Practices in the Implementation of Mid-Day Meal Programme in Karnataka. National University of Educational Planning and Administration, 2008.

Subudhi, S.C. (2013). "Free Food Facility at Elementary School: Towards Rural Educational Empowerment in Meghalaya", Anweshan Journal of Education, Vol.II& III, No.2&1, pp.55-60.

Swain, B.C. &Sahu, A.N. (2014). "Mid-Day Meal Programme in the Primary Schools of Odisha: An Evaluative Study", Anweshan Journal of Education. Vol.III,No. 2 and Vol. IV, No.1, pp. 55-65.

Swain, B.C. (2008). "Mid-Day Meal Programme in Primary Schools: A Study", Journal of Board of Secondary Education, Odisha.

Swain, B.C. and Sahu, A.N. (2010). "Mid-Day Meal Programme: Its Impact & Status", VivekInternational Journal of Education and Research, Vol.1, No.3, pp. 49-51.

Websites

https://www.akshayapatra.org/

https://timesofindia.indiatimes.com

https://mdm.gujarat.gov.in/

www.mdm.nic.in